AF473713

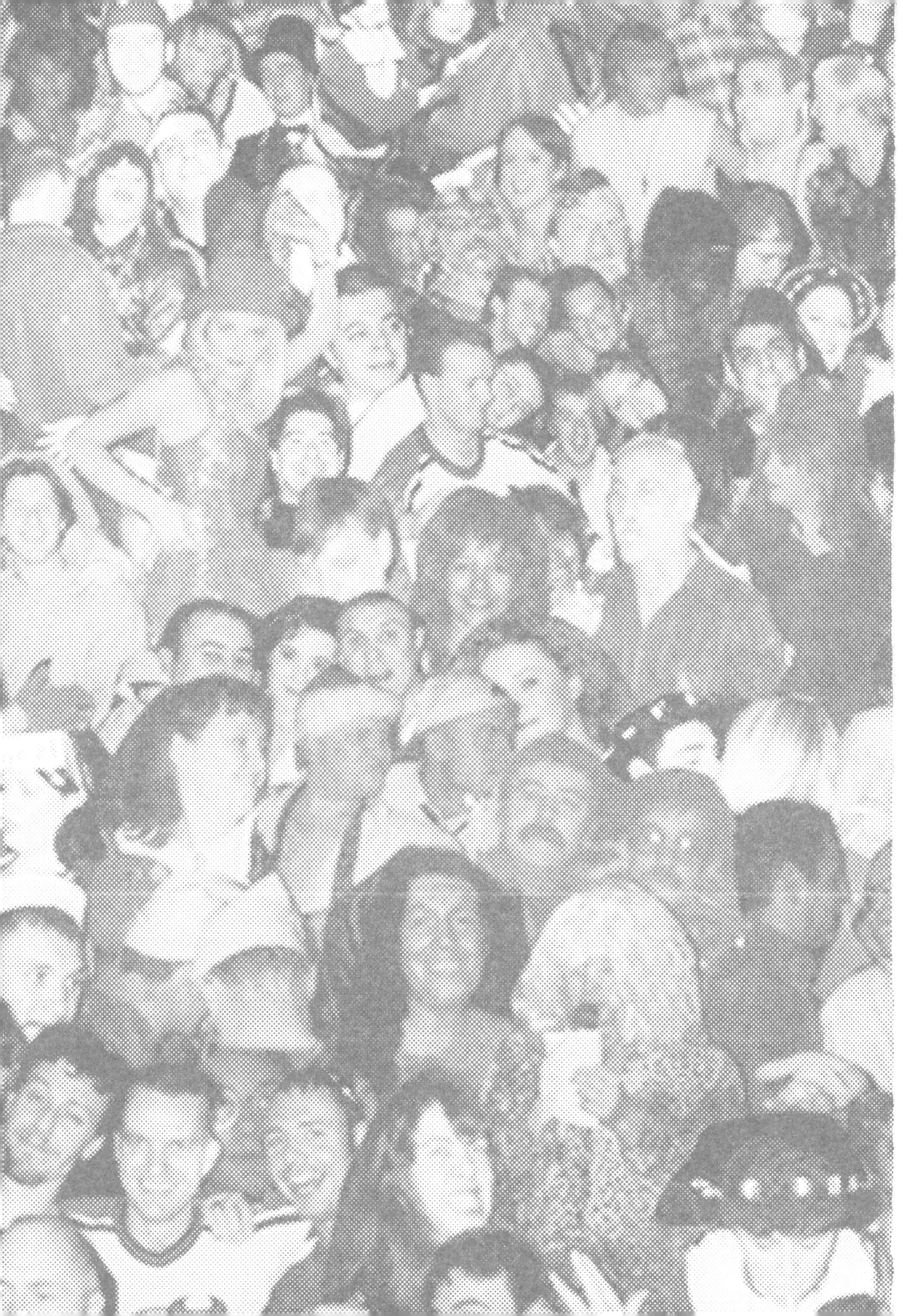

Richard Hughes

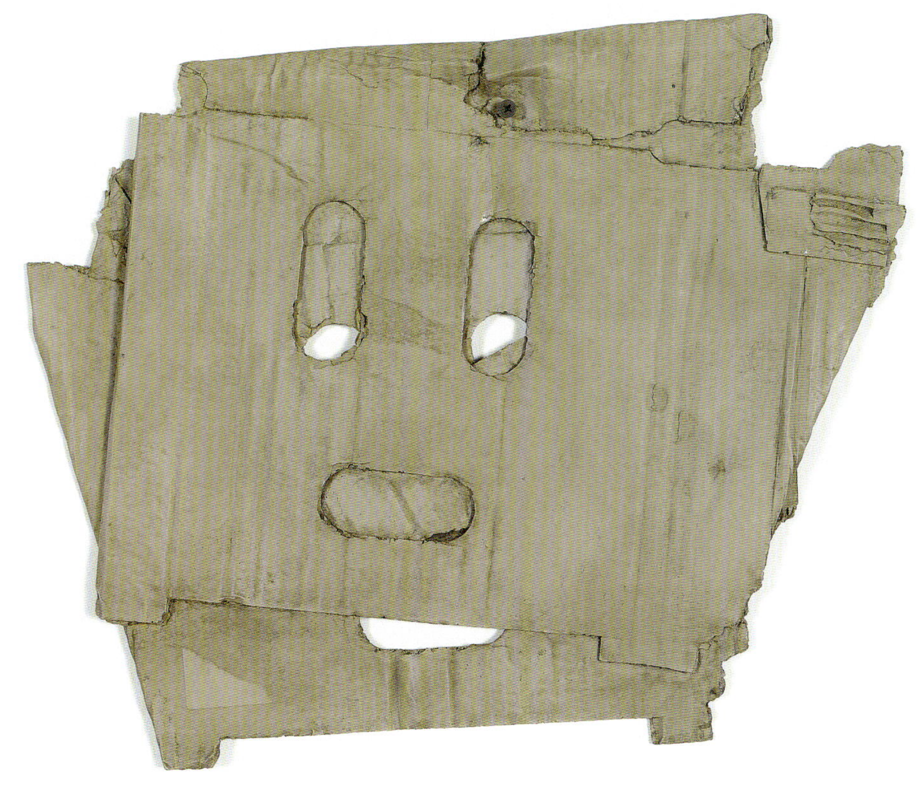

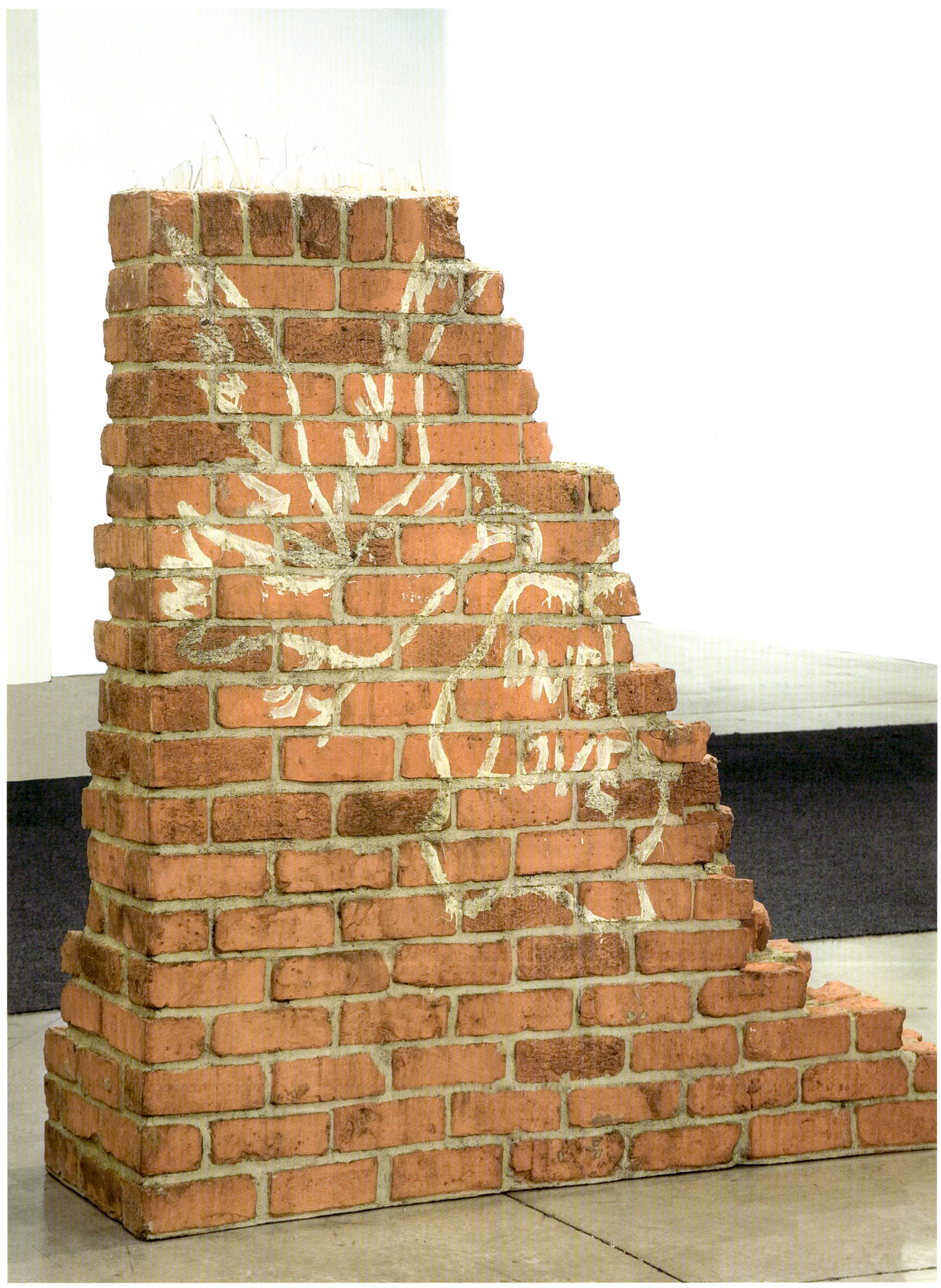

MASK, 2011
←

DIAMOND DUST, 2010

Somniloquy
Joanne Tatham

I had to build this wall and I thought if I tried to lay the bricks, I'd spend so much time trying to lay them right, I thought I'll get someone who's a brickie, so he was doing the laying and the whistling. What I had to do then, once that was done, I made a mould of it and that was the time consuming bit really.

All that stuff is in the work, it's all true. It's not that it isn't true, but there's this thing, I'm not sure what it is, but this thing that is being skirted around. You can talk about it like this or you can find the right word for that.

About the wall, what should be said about the wall. I shouldn't even call it a wall. It's not a wall. I wouldn't call it a wall.

It's like there was one thing, the first thing and that was a new piece of writing. Since then, it all comes out from there. I'd like to get it all together. Each piece of writing is a copy! I'd like to get it all together. Put all of it together somehow, you know, trace the words back to the source.

Then there's another piece. A tree!

I mean you can almost kid yourself that there is some element of possibility, that it's real or it's found and then as soon as you add a light to it, it's like it's from a pound shop! You can't believe in it! You can call it a wall but that won't make it a wall. I can show you a tree. I can show you a face.

A lot of the stuff just tends to … It does just tend to … I feel a lot like that about my works … My attachment to them feels a bit second-hand sometimes, it's done and it's gone. You spend so long with them … I feel a funny kind of relationship to them sometimes. You spend so long with them … and then they leave. You can enjoy looking at it for about 10 minutes before it gets put in a van and taken away.

The corporeal body that was one, one of those words at college. Entropy was also quite popular. It's a relevant state to be aware of! I'm not going to write a dissertation on it. Or the other thing of course. It's the high art equivalent blah … blah … You know, the skateboard flips. It used to drive me bananas.

There's been one or two times that I've made a mould of something, then either had a u-turn and think it's not quite right and that's the only time when things stay around really. Or times when your broken stuff comes back. That's happened quite a bit. There's a shelf of things that need to get repaired. It's quite depressing.

Moulds take up a bit of space. I try to keep a mould for a couple of years usually, in case there has to be a repair, the times when your broken stuff comes back. I'm reluctant to chuck them, the amount of money rubber costs, it costs hundreds and hundreds. I've got a shed at home that is just packed with old moulds. They take up a quite a bit of space the moulds.

Where I grew up, it's not that bad. It was on the edges of B_, but that's almost irrelevant. It's not like I grew up on the moon and it was made of cheese! That's not really my thing.

No I wouldn't do a show based on a specific interest. I'm not capable of making that kind of work. I don't have any authority on anything. I shoved those things in the corner intentionally. It looked like the work hadn't arrived.

Mind you the stories of the work are so anecdotal at times, they take you for a ride right round the block! It's almost irrelevant.

The story was my cousin was in a band and they weren't very good. Every year he used to send us one of his records. Apparently they were big in Portugal or Greece, but I doubt that. Then my cousin decided he was into The Doors and he recorded this song as a tribute to Jim Morrison. That's where the title for that comes from. The band was called Dizzy Heights. Then all of a sudden my cousin decided that he was some kind of authority on Jim Morrison and he did this track as a tribute. The whole song was full of Doors quotes. That's where the title for that comes from.

The abject. There's another one. I'm not going to write a dissertation on it. The way I see it, the way I tell it, is like this. When I make a work I use all my skills to decide what to do next. That's how the work gets made. I don't write something on a piece of paper and hide it inside. When it's finished, I don't whisper in its ear! I'm quite sentimental I suppose but my attachment to it feels a bit second-hand sometimes, it's done and it's gone.

There's nothing scientific about it, it's just labour and it's technique. I'm satisfied I get to the end though, when you get to the end and you can go, yeah that's achieved what I set out to do. You can enjoy looking at it for about 10 minutes before it gets put in a van and taken away. Sometimes they take you for a ride right round the block!

When it's finished I don't whisper in its ear. I don't write something on a piece of paper and hide it inside. Sometimes it's not a word that I like but the stance that it takes, yeah, not in terms of physically its pose or its gesture. I am aware of putting things in a sort of position where they are awkward or clumsy … I shoved those things in the corner intentionally. I've never been someone who is in the spotlight but the thing that I really like is letting the things do the talking.

I did have a proposal ... I did make a broken cat, I got a black cat and smashed it up and then remade it bit by bit. It was never going to work, it was an exercise in failure.

SHUT DOWN 2, 2010

Now I have a lot of time to consider, you know, when you have a lot of time to consider ... Now I think about one piece and one title and it still takes me ages to find a title if they don't come naturally. I will be ideally reading something, just looking for things. Sometimes I just forget them.

I wanted to be an artist since I was young, or a hairdresser. The harder I thought about it ... it was really killing the work, so I stopped.

Then there's another piece I made. The bike ... that got taken away. They went right round the block with that! That's what the work does, that's its function ... but just to be able to do that. It seems quite pathetic, but it means quite a lot really.

The more I thought about it the harder it was getting. There are certain things that I do ... You erase your interests and think about things that you are just drawn to. In the end I should have just written I make some stuff. Then there are some things I never even ask about. It's almost irrelevant. Yeah, I'm going to have to lose a lot of stuff. I think we have to find some way of ordering these things together.

I've done a lot of casts from cardboard. I made 20 to 30 pieces that have been various crushed boxes and flattened things, but once they start to get put all together it's sort of ... ha ha, you can have too much of a good thing! In a way that might be the best way of doing it. Then there are the slightly anthropomorphic pieces. Another is broken bits. Or go from light brown to dark brown.

It's like with this book. There's got to be some way of making sense of it. That's as far as we've got, we're faced with hundreds and hundreds of pictures. It's just like a massive messy scrapbook, in my head it is anyway! It drives me bananas. I'll give my Mum a copy. She'll just say that's lovely. She won't read it. My dad will have a flick through it. It's not something you have much say over when you're growing up is it?

I suppose the labour aspect of it all, I'm doing everything by myself, so you pick up ways and tricks and techniques and there are probably people, professionals, who know these things a lot better ... But I don't suppose it is about control or anything ... Yeah, it's just a job.

Now I forget my titles and things ... I was making these bottles and I was thinking they might lead somewhere. Because they are quite labour intensive and I can't cut corners on them and I do have to spend a lot of hours on them. I'd rather it wasn't that way. If I did have a lot of money, I don't know if I'd ... Then there was this other piece I made. I made a clock. Well, I say it was a clock, it didn't tell you the time! Ha ha. It was one of those ones.

There's this other one here. What is that? I can't remember what I called it and it's like my favourite thing that I've made all year! I was thinking to myself last night what the bloody hell did I call that piece. I end up describing it and that's awful. I shouldn't do that and it's always the ones that get taken away as well, I find. The van comes to pick them up and they get taken away.

When it comes to the painting, I take real pride in that, it's quite satisfying. When it comes to the finish, those are the things that make me continue making the type of work that I do ... That's one of the great things about calling yourself an artist, not that I'm going to wear crazy glasses or something, but that you could get away with it, you know. That's important to me. I make stuff and I don't write something on a piece of paper and hide it inside. When it's finished, I don't whisper in its ear.

Something like fibreglass that isn't expensive. The bronze for the small things, I used it for its resilience. There is something about painted bronze, these spit balls, there's something quite beautiful about that. I shoved those in the corner. It looked like the work hadn't arrived.

I wouldn't quite say natural, but there is a naturalism to it, you know what I mean. I have to be very careful where I put things. It might be something like the way that you look at it as a viewer, it might be something that you use as an angle to view something ... I'm not like an inch that way, one more, no stop. It drives me bananas!

You can kid yourself that it's real but then it's like it's from a pound shop! You can't believe in it. There was the wood as well, wasn't there, the burning wood. I shouldn't even call it that, I shouldn't even say that!

Yeah, it's just a job. I'd definitely have someone doing the mould making because it's not something I get satisfaction from. I know I can make a mould properly, which is good to know, but it is so fucking boring, I get no pleasure. I wasn't up in arms about it, I just thought, well that's kind of the way that I work, you have a way of working and you just do it.

Well you have to make a living out of it. There's a shelf of things that need to get repaired. It's quite depressing. I try to keep a mould for a couple of years usually in case there has to be a repair, the times when your broken stuff comes back. Moulds take up a bit of space! I've got a shed at home that is just packed with old moulds.

The making is one part of it that you have to go through, but the way they behave, yes that's very important ... A lot of the stuff just tends to ... it does just tend to ... I feel a lot like that about my works ... My attachment to them feels a bit second-hand sometimes, it's done and it's gone. You spend so long with them ... And then they leave. You can enjoy looking at it for about 10 minutes before it gets put in a van and taken away. Yeah, it gets put in a van and sometimes they take it right round the block.

SHUT DOWN 1, 2010

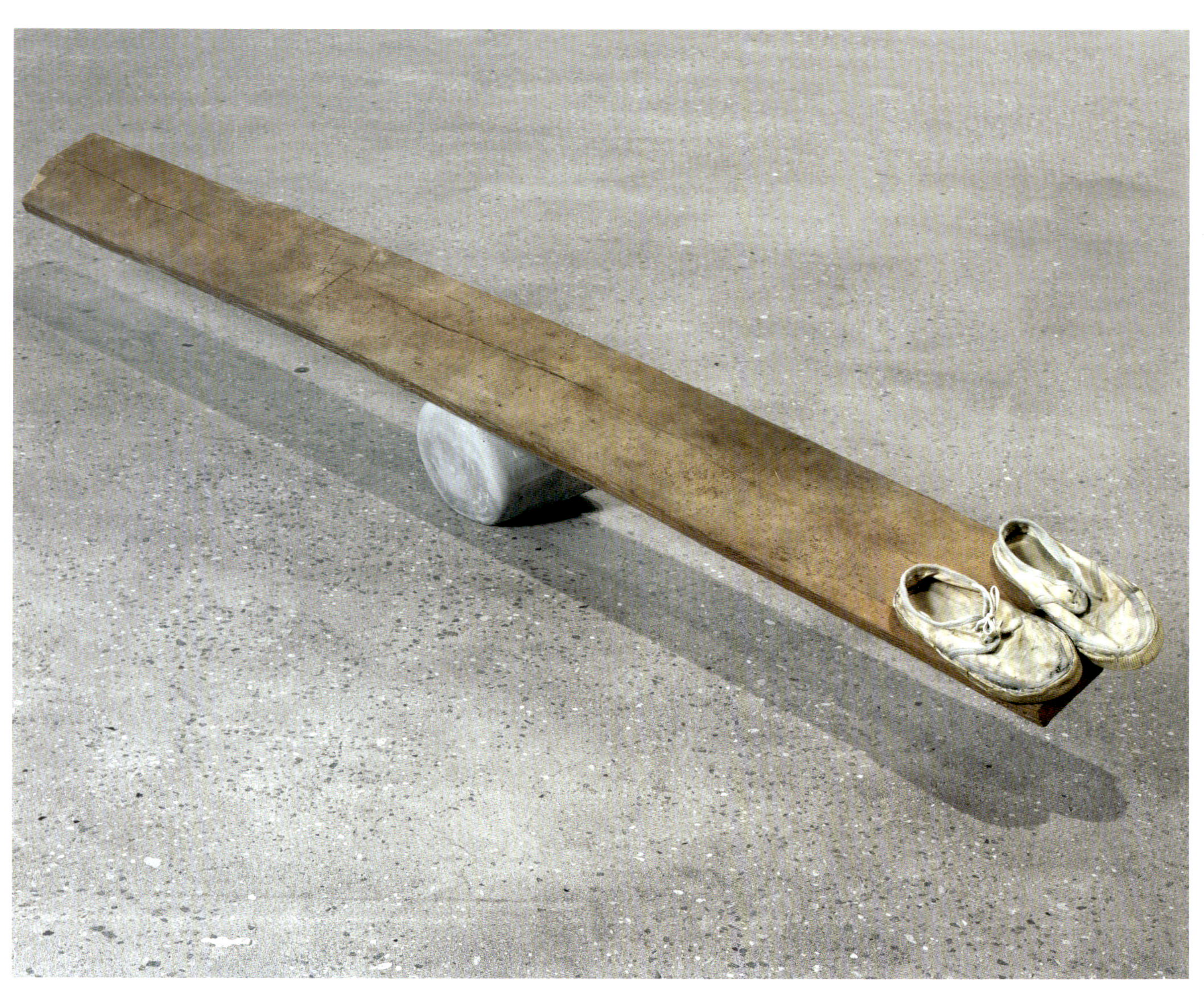

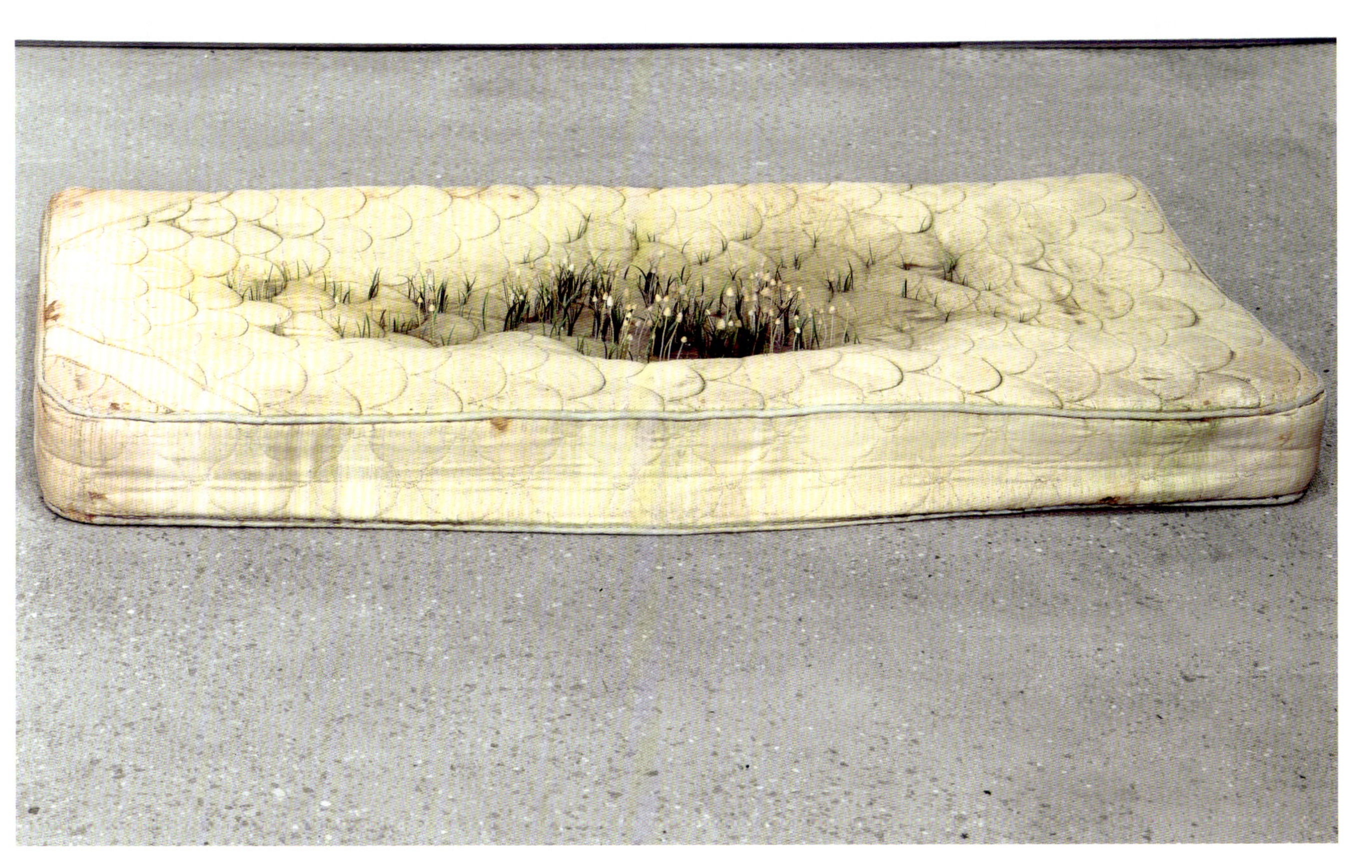

THE BIG SLEEP, 2007

THE MALINGERER, 2010, detail

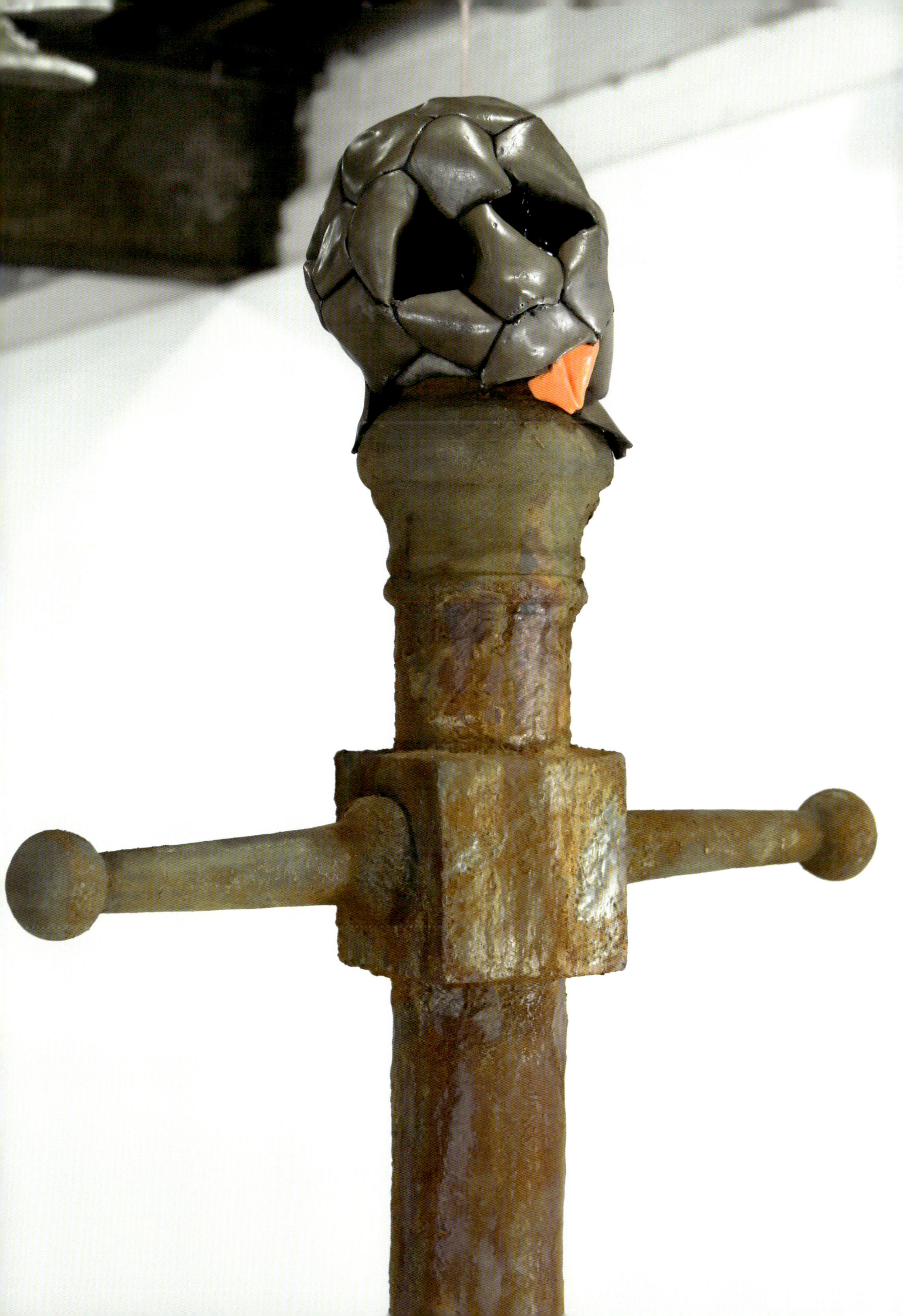

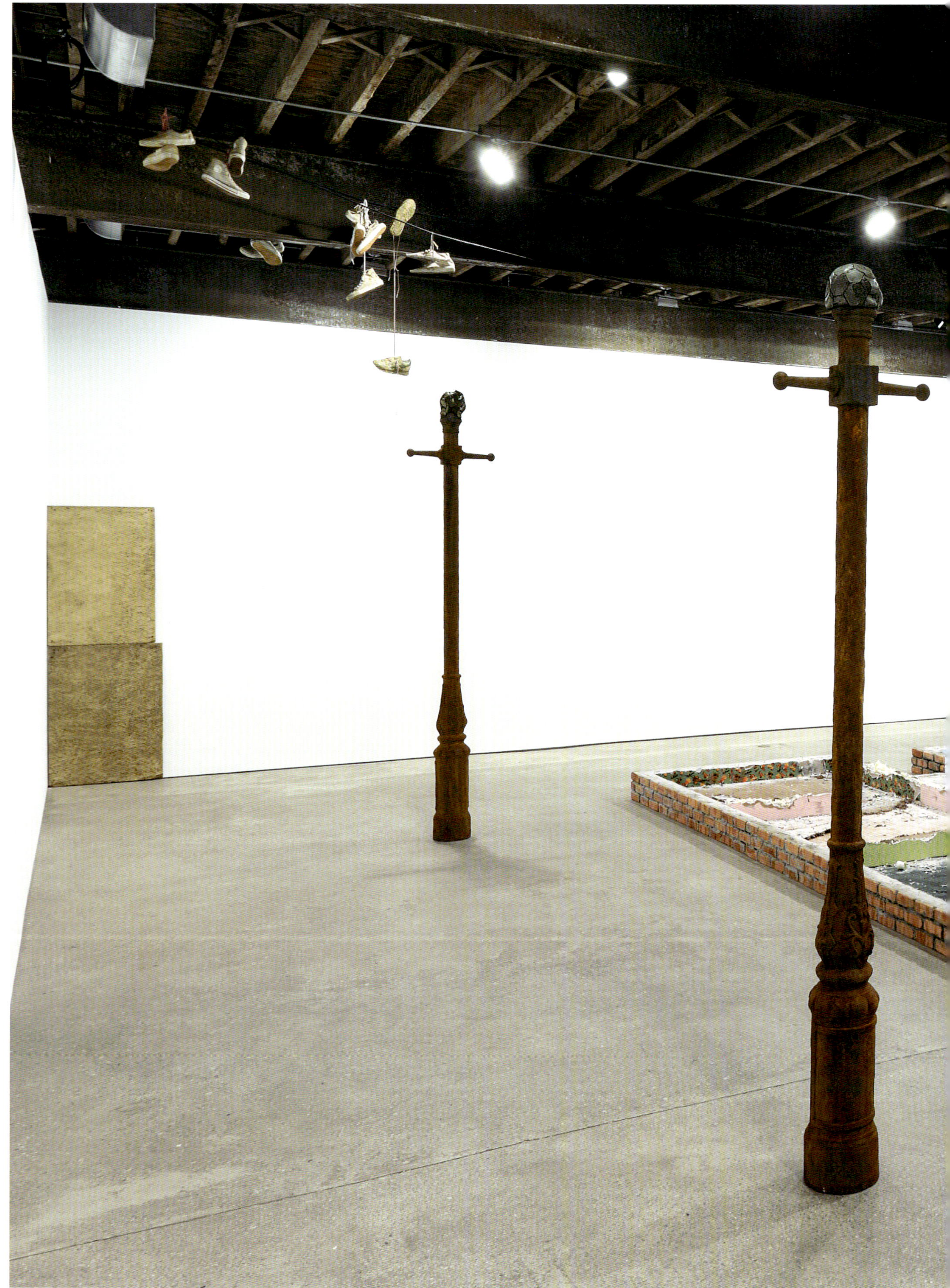

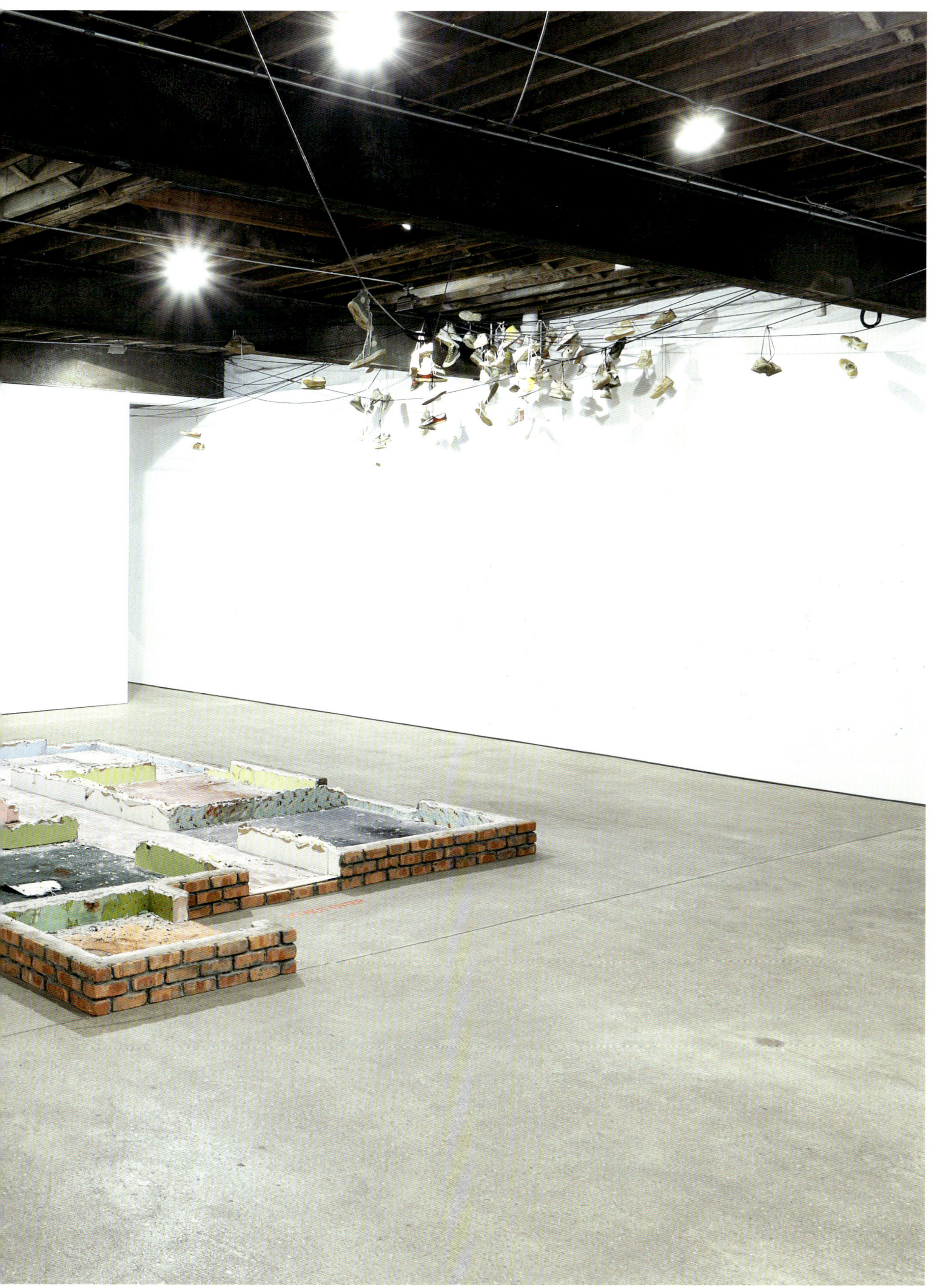

Installation view, Anton Kern Gallery, New York, 2010

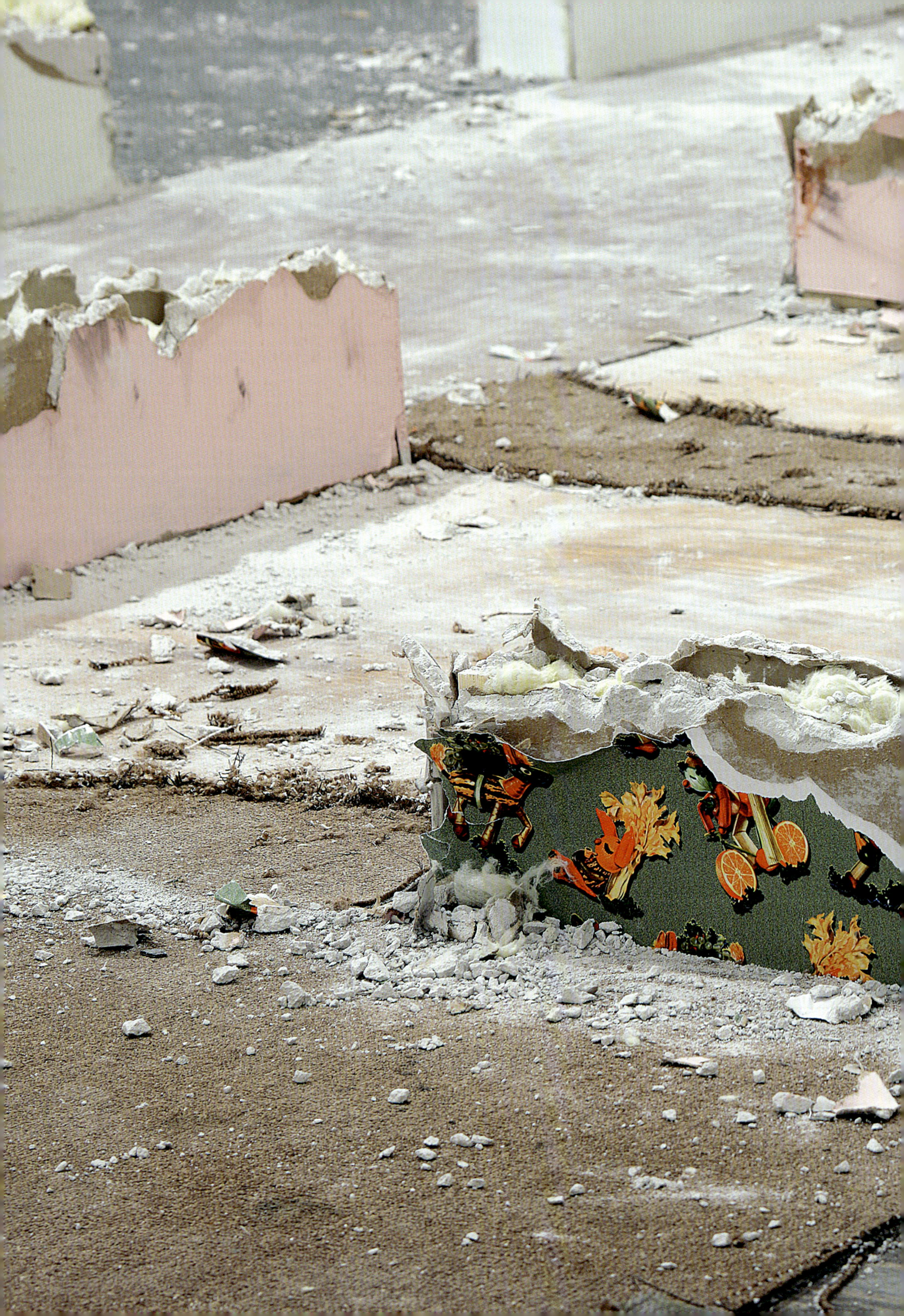

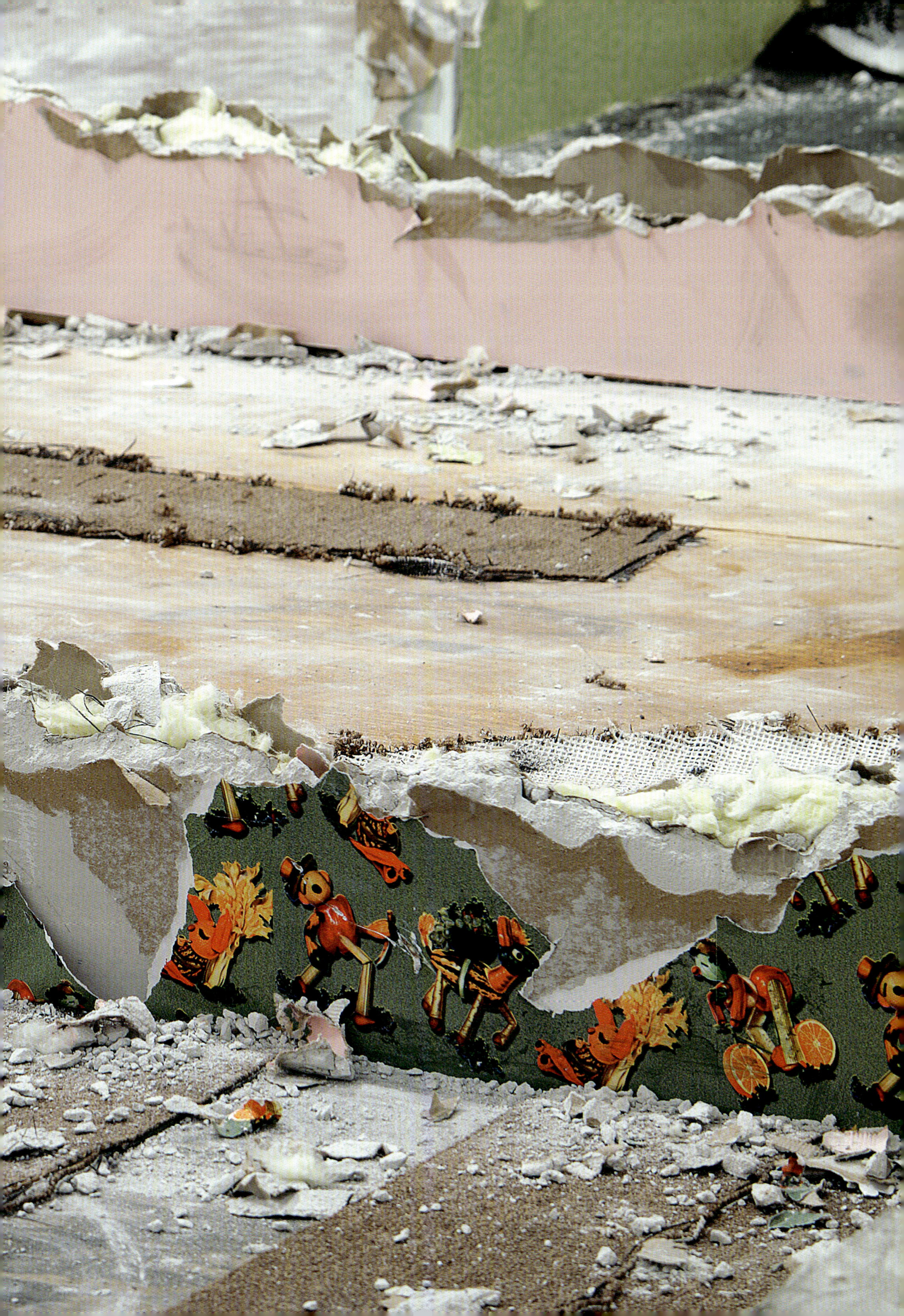

JIMMY, JIMMY (THE END), 2010, detail
←

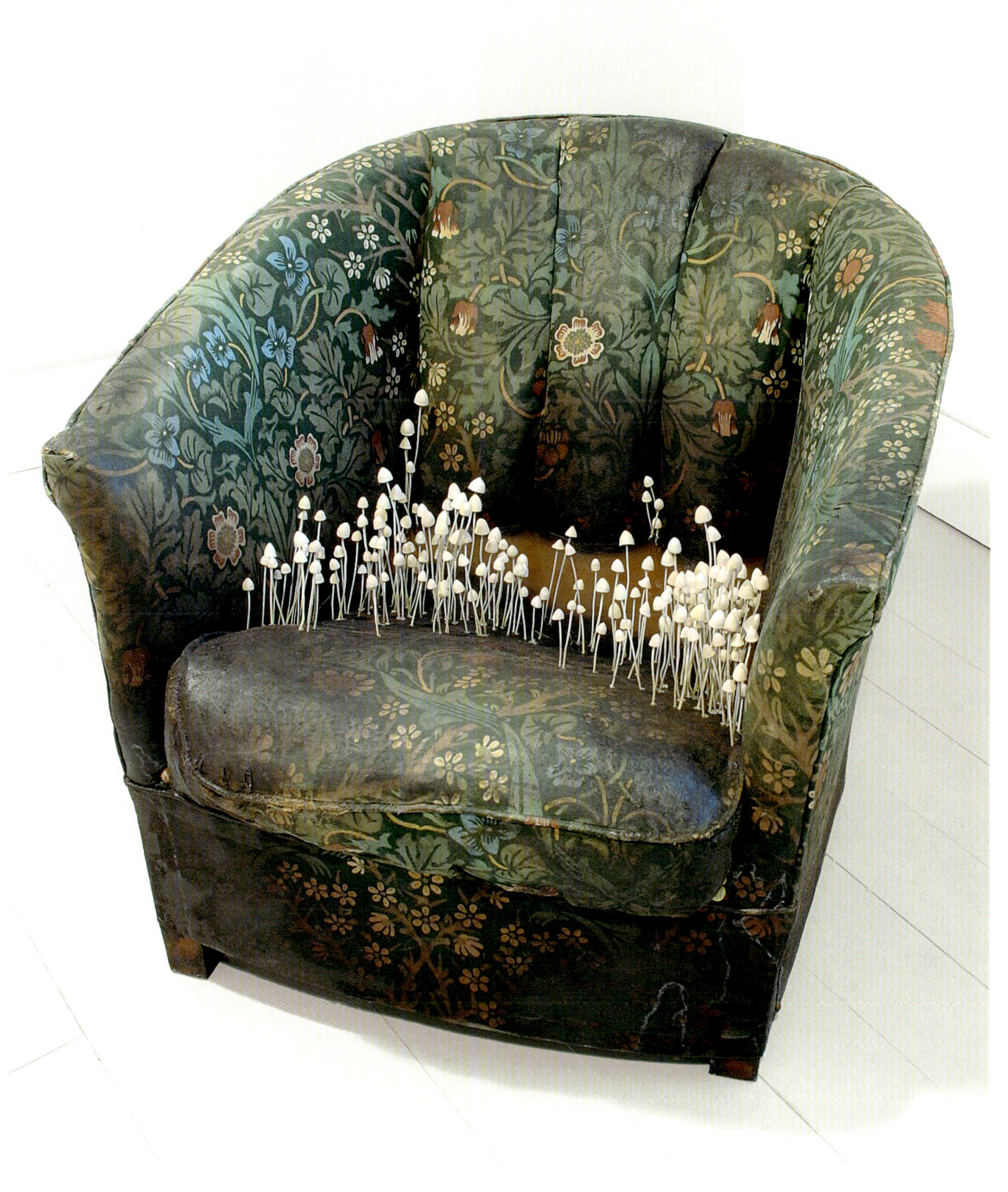

DEEPENDING, 2006

WE'RE ALL MAD, 2008
→

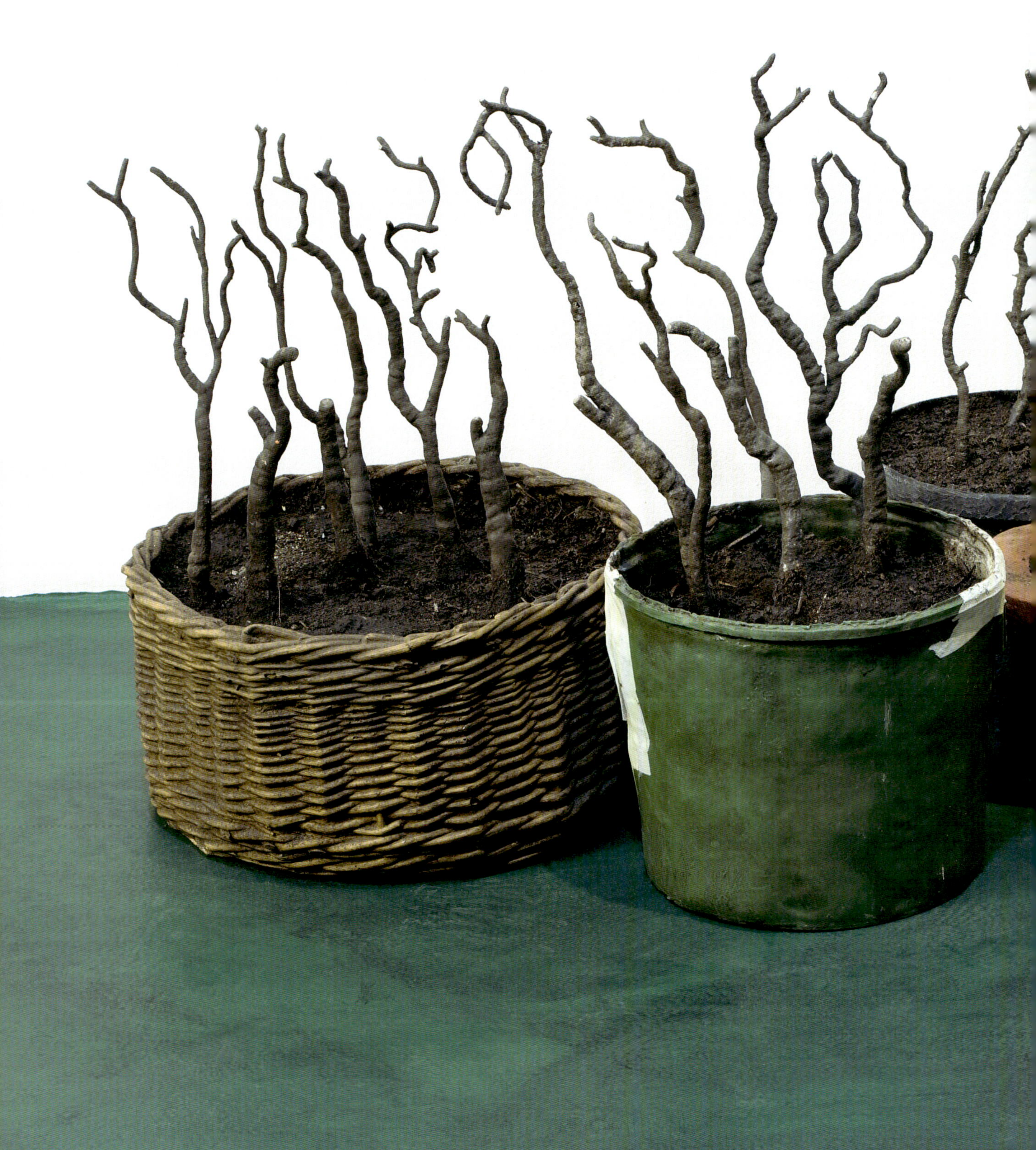

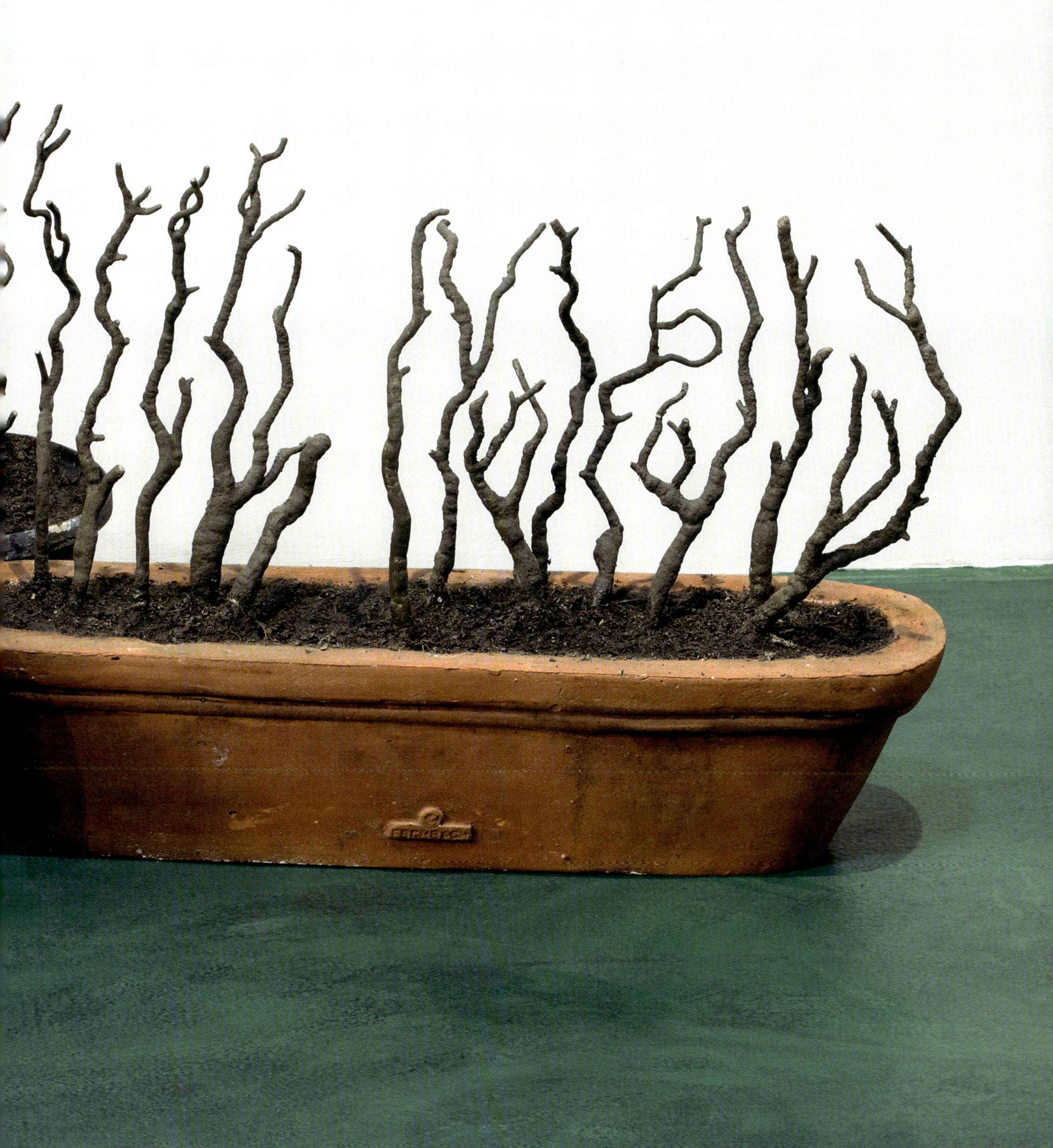

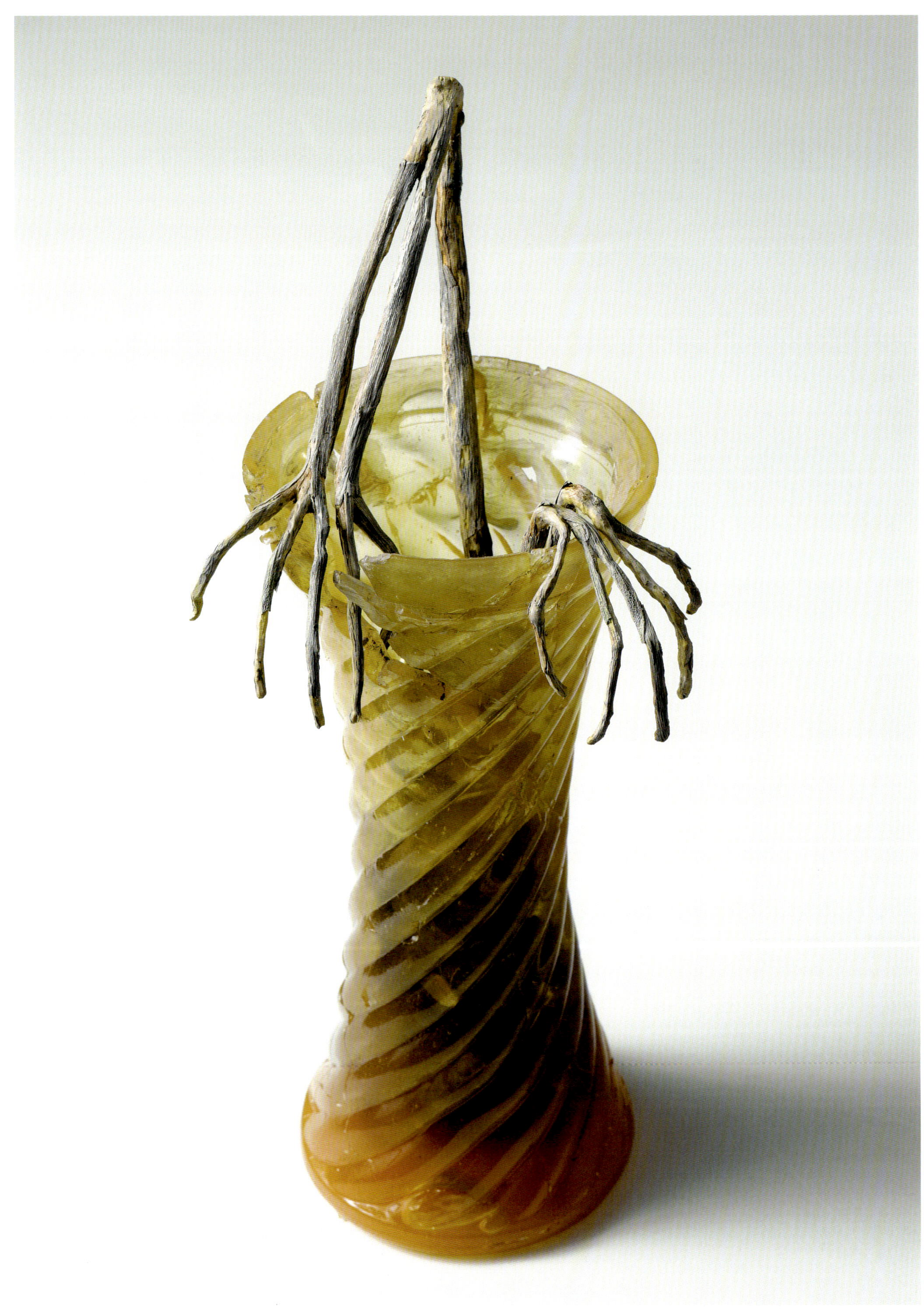

GHOST PAW, 2006

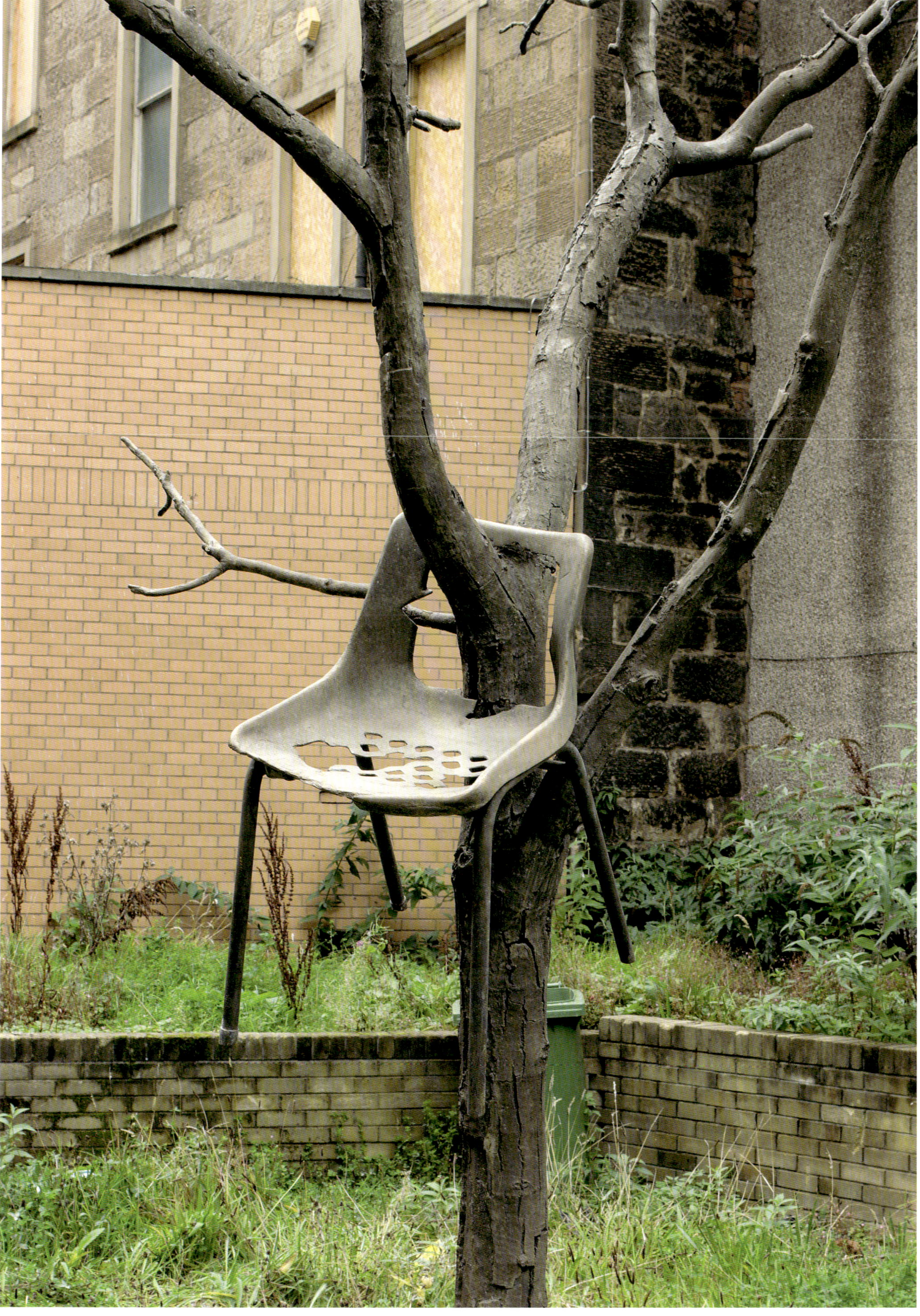

IT IS NEVER TOO LATE TO BECOME WHAT YOU MIGHT HAVE BEEN, 2008, detail

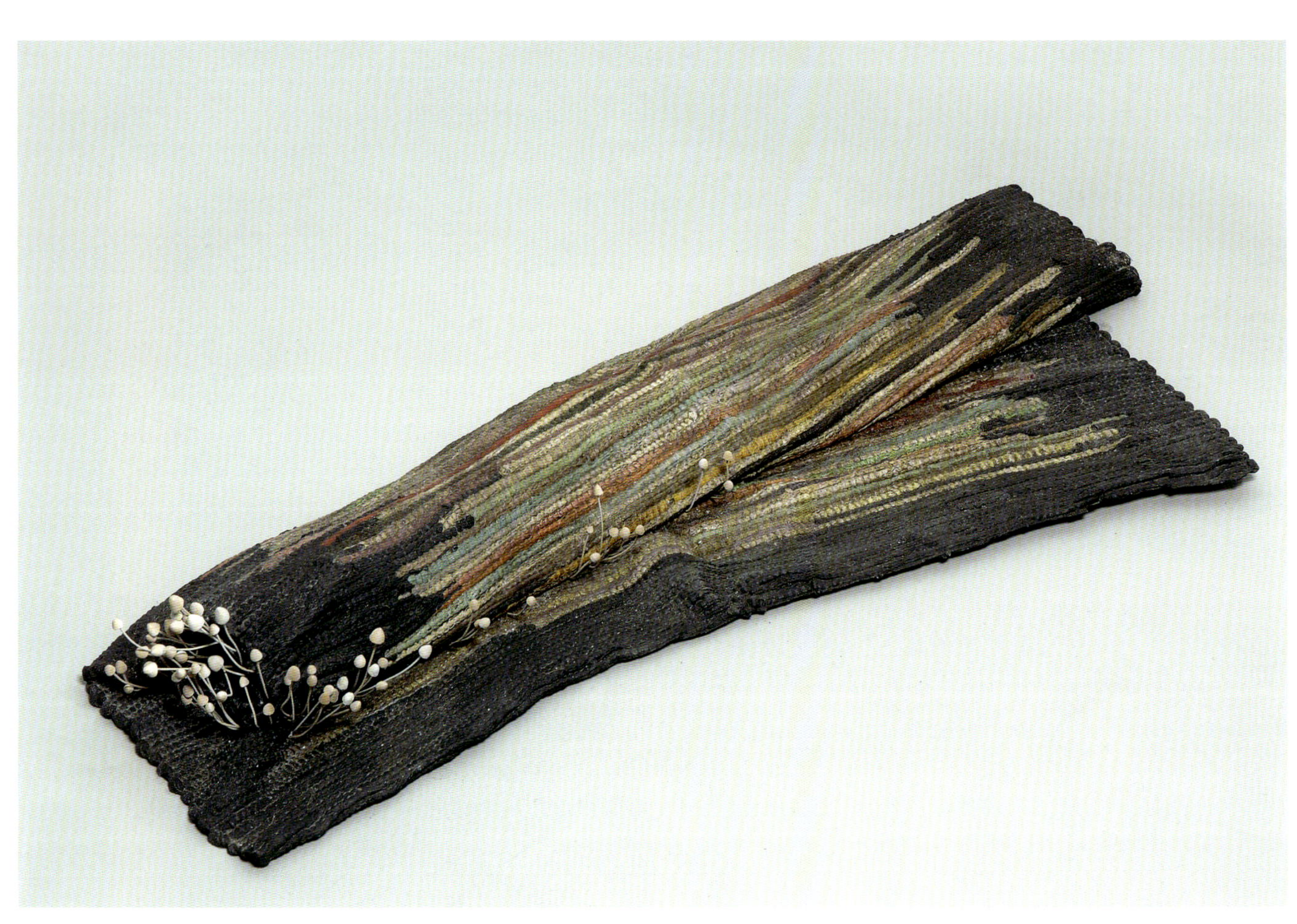

UNTITLED, 2007

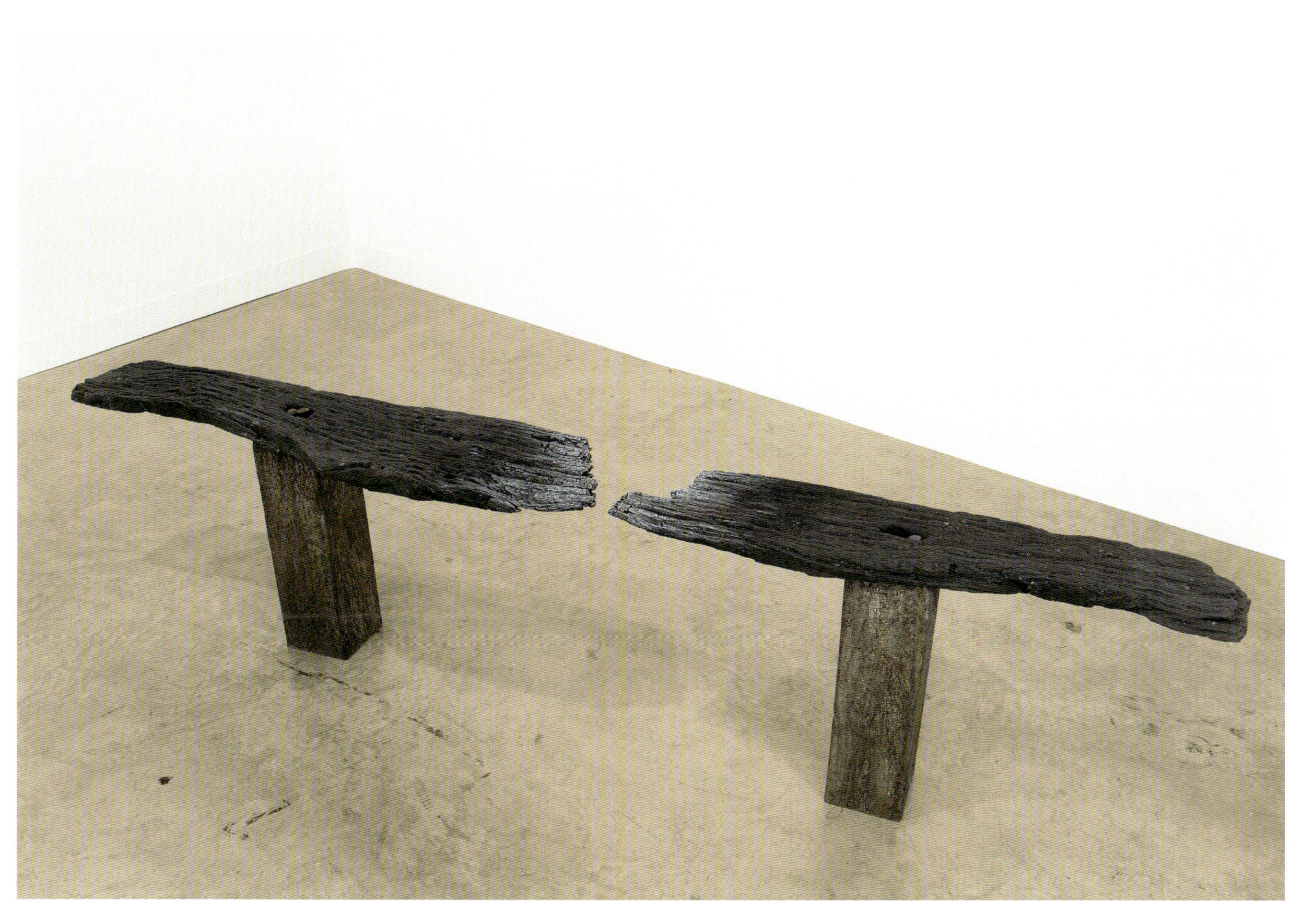

WOT WE DID ON OUR HOLIDAYS, 2010

WOT WE DID ON OUR HOLIDAYS, 2010, detail
→

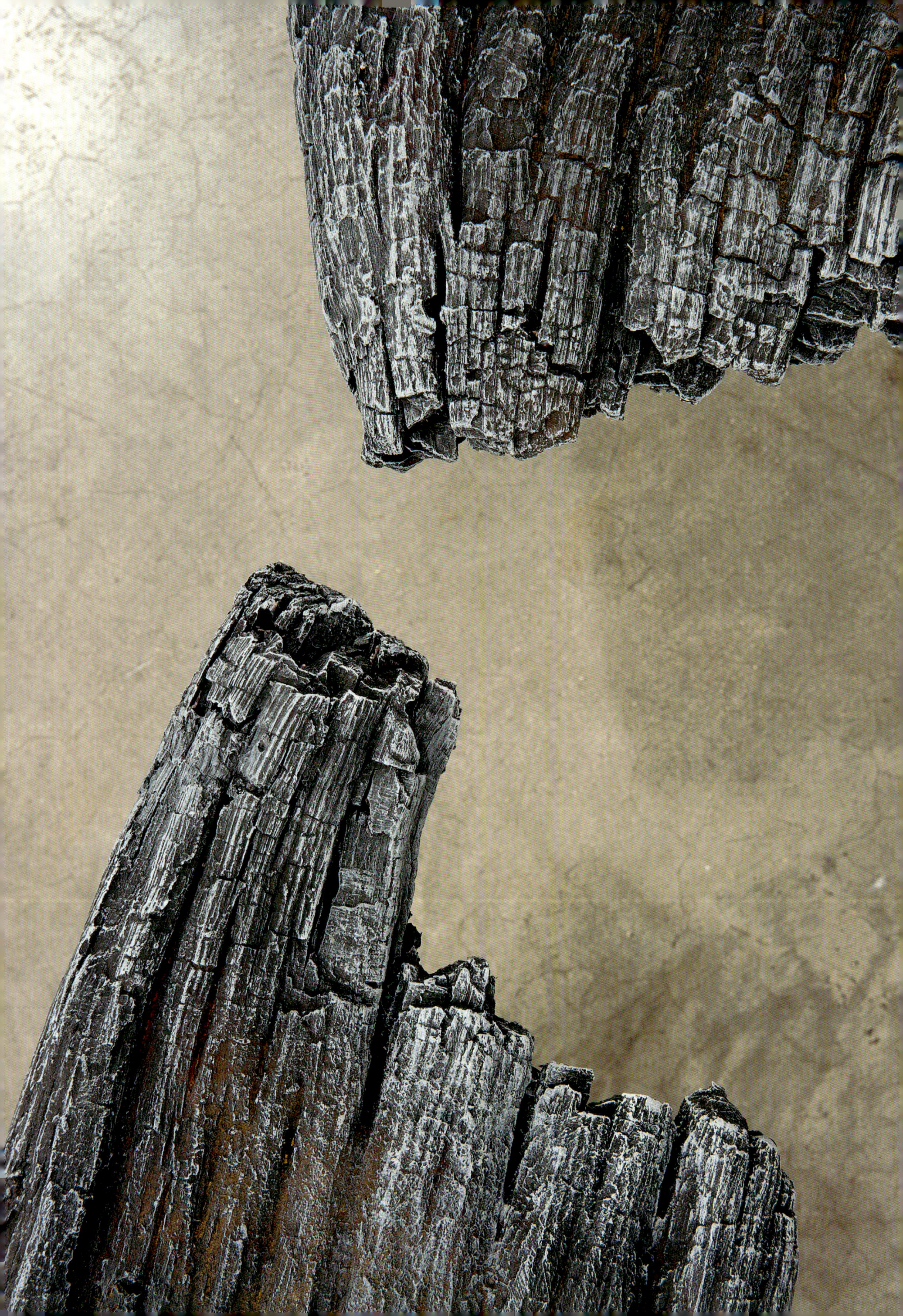

"You'll be dead for years and you won't even know it"
Richard Hughes in Conversation with Martin Clark

MARTIN CLARK I wanted to start by asking you why you began to make sculpture?

RICHARD HUGHES That's a good start, the big one. When I was on my first degree at Staffordshire University, Stoke, I based myself in the painting department, but that probably had more to do with wanting to engage with certain staff members there. They had an approach where they would encourage you to use external facilities, you know, to actually realise what you wanted to do as a normal part of artistic practice. I began to get some small bits and pieces made: vacuum-formed parts, printed material, rosettes and other tat. Very early on I became interested in this idea of not using found or existing objects, but of making something that looked like it could have been lifted from the real world. I guess it was jointly down to a lack of funds, as well as a sense of pride in craftsmanship. So there was already this need to reproduce from what was around me. I never had any desire to be a sculptor in terms of more formal concerns – materiality, physicality, space – all the stuff that at the time I associated with making sculpture. It was more a means to an end, making objects was about my interest in engaging with things, trying to get some kind of authenticity.

MARTIN CLARK You've talked to me before about process being really important for you. Is that where it starts, in the making?

RICHARD HUGHES Early on I had to pick up techniques from scratch, like casting or mould-making, and at first there was a kind of fascination with them, a seduction about what I could do. I became more and more obsessed with those processes, with getting it really exact. Day-to-day, the making process can be a pretty drawn out and repetitive job, but it gives you a very intimate knowledge of an object. You develop that through every stage, from choosing the object, reproducing it, fabricating it, finishing it, and that's become an important part of the work, that time spent in making.

MARTIN CLARK There's definitely a very strong sense of labour invested in your works. I know you very rarely use assistants to help with fabrication and that seems important in your work in a way that it wouldn't necessarily be in another artists' work.

RICHARD HUGHES I've only had a handful of things professionally fabricated, often that's using materials I can't manipulate myself, although now and again it's been to ease the burden of getting things done on time. But I tend to limit that to the very straightforward processes, the mould making or whatever. When it comes to finishing, a lot of the time I simply trust what I can do more than someone else. If it messes up it's down to me. It's the part of my practice that I get real satisfaction from, and that I can get lost in. But again it's about the value of spending time with the object. It's a pretty solitary activity for me and I think that invests something very intimate in the work that wouldn't be there if I used assistants.

MARTIN CLARK There seems to be an important relationship, or tension maybe, between that investment you make in recreating or reproducing something – the time and labour and attention required in that – and the particular nature of the things you choose to work with. You're often drawn to very modest or overlooked objects, things that are worn out, used up, spent, but which you reclaim or rescue in a way. It's initially enacted through your selection of them, bringing them back to the light as it were, but it's then amplified through that process of painstakingly, perhaps lovingly, reproducing them.

RICHARD HUGHES I think that's right. I'd rather the objects I find had some sort of past life. Not that I'm particularly drawn to exactly what each specific object did before, it's more the fact that they have reached this state of uselessness, and how well they can be used now to deliver a narrative or depict something.

MARTIN CLARK They often have a very strong relationship to the body. Whether that's through their relationship to the world of utility and use, or to the fact that some of them become quite anthropomorphic: whether that's a speaker with a T-shirt stretched over it to make a kind of odd torso (*Small Town Big Man*, 2011), or a bundle of old clothes that are arranged to evoke a hand or a face (*Love Seat*, 2005).

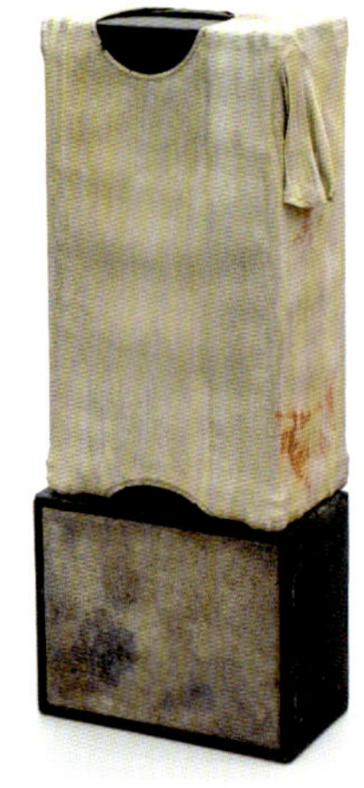

SMALL TOWN BIG MAN, 2011

RICHARD HUGHES There's a need for balance within these pieces. If it's something that's already slightly anthropomorphic I have to somehow reign that in a little so it doesn't look too contrived. I want it to look as if it could almost have occurred naturally or by chance, rather than having been made or created. If it does look like it's been purposefully manipulated, I tend to contextualise it within some kind of framework or narrative that suggests someone else might have placed or arranged it to give it meaning, or that it was the result of some sort of anonymous gesture, of bravado perhaps, or laziness: like someone throwing something over a lamppost, or a discarded pile of local newspapers (*Untitled (Wasted Youth)*, 2009). Domestic situations like the speaker with the T-shirt on, that's actually from an anecdotal story about my brother-in-law buying a Gary Moore concert T-shirt that was too small for him, so he put it on his amp and there it stayed for eight years, never worn, but hideously misshapen. I choose these kinds of objects partly because of that history of use, the fact that they are proximal objects – they've been in contact with bodies – but also because they've usually reached the end of any useful life and have become, essentially, undesirables. The casting and fabricating process these objects undergo allows me, within my reconstructions, to trap them in that liminal state, in-between two opposing situations.

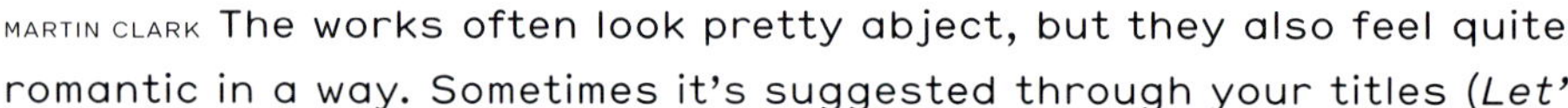

MARTIN CLARK The works often look pretty abject, but they also feel quite romantic in a way. Sometimes it's suggested through your titles (*Let's*

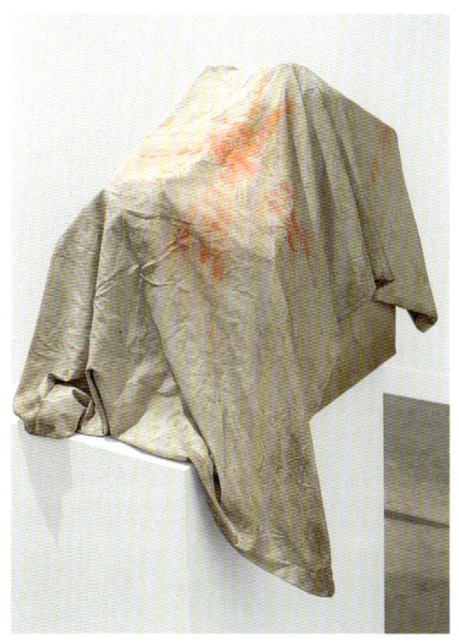

MONDAY MOURNING, 2011

not and say we did, 2003) which are always great, but there's also a sense of pathos inherent in many of these objects, despite, or perhaps because of, their dilapidation or 'base' nature.

RICHARD HUGHES I think I'm massively sentimental. I didn't used to think I was, you know, making these decrepit, broken, found looking things. I guess that I was initially taking this anti-heroic stance, and that was possibly a reaction to what I saw going on in the art world when I was doing my MA at Goldsmiths in 2002. But I think in my work there's always this idea of me trying to free something from my own past. In one way or another I'm illustrating an attachment to a time and place that's really specific to me. I've since found that these things are actually far more universal, but I began thinking they belonged exclusively to the kind of background I had and the cities I've lived in. I seem to return to that period more and more, not a particular cultural period, but that time in my life when I spent hours in these shut down shopping precincts and car parks – I was a skateboarder – and I must think back on that as a golden era. I've mixed it up with all the things that were references to my life at that time.

MARTIN CLARK As children or young people we seem to inhabit these liminal spaces, particularly in early adolescence, when you're caught between childhood and the world of adults. You can go off to the shopping centre on your own, but you don't have any money to spend there, so you can't use it in the way that it's been designed to be used, you can't 'shop' as it were. Instead you just sort of hang around, and that hanging around leads to you seeing and experiencing those places in a totally different way. If you are taken to the pub by your parents, you're not allowed in, instead you're outside with a Coke and a packet of crisps, looking at the brick wall or the bit by the bins, inhabiting and observing the space of all the stuff that everyone else walks past, that's invisible to them. I think it's a really powerful time in terms of the way we experience the materiality and specificity of the world. It's lost as you become an adult because the world then opens towards you, gathers you in, and it sort of disappears in a sense – or these in-between spaces and the stuff that collects in them does.

RICHARD HUGHES It also leads to a kind of make-do ethos. I was too young for punk but my oldest brother was into it, and I'd see him making his own clothes. Then he got into Mod and he'd design these jumpers for my Nan to knit. You know, you couldn't afford to buy them so you'd make do. I had skate shorts made from my Nan's nylon trousers ... They did just look like my Nan's trousers though!

MARTIN CLARK It's that idea of the replica again, but I'm interested in the references to subcultures as well. A number of people have spoken about how your work invokes various subcultures, but they always seem to be filtered through a very specific, British experience. So although we talked about the universality of many of these images and ideas, there's a sense in your work that they're already second-hand by the time they get to you. Whether it's American West Coast skate culture or hippy psychedelia, it's already a replicated or bootlegged version

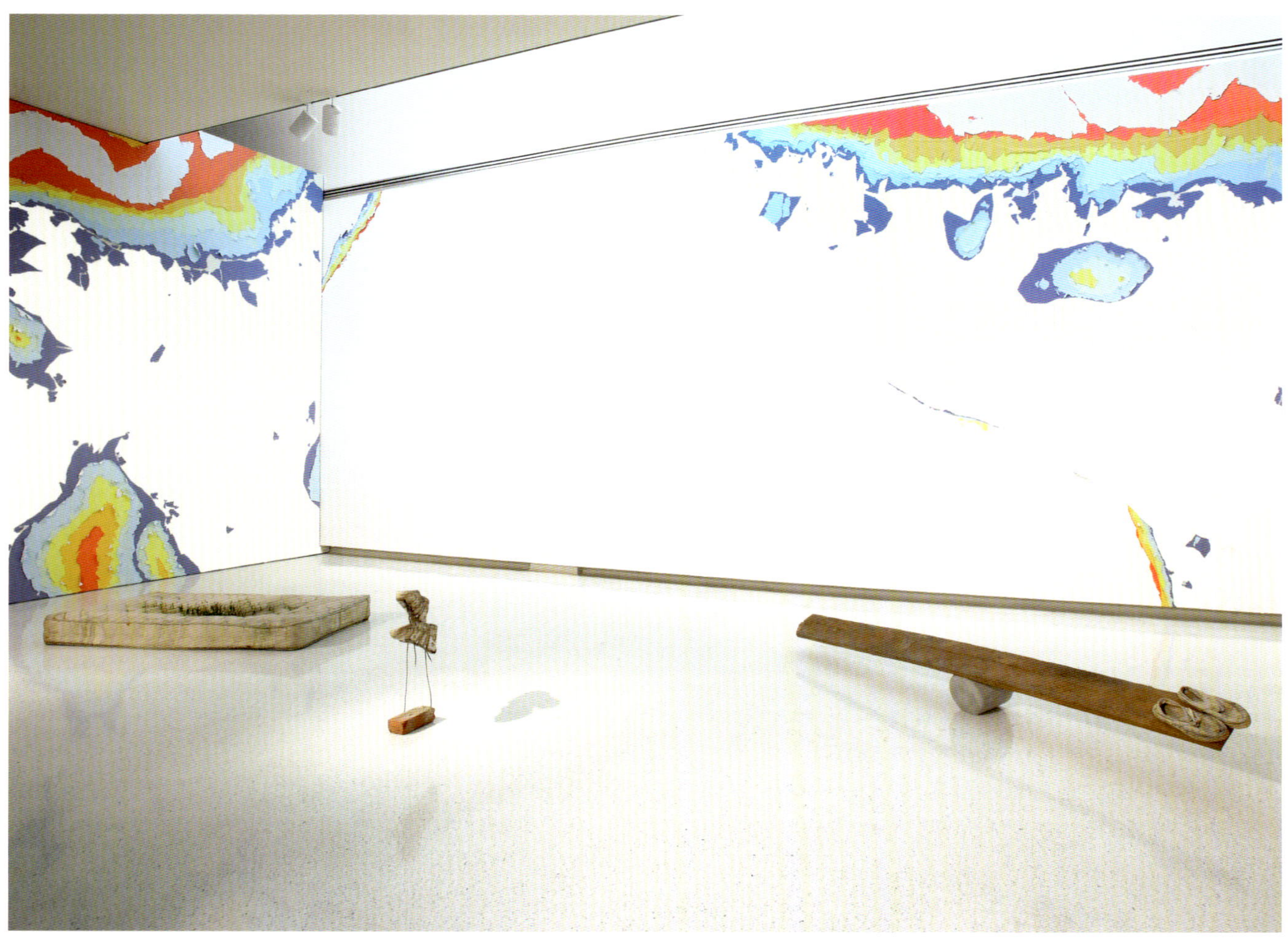

Installation view, LIFE ON MARS, 55th Carnegie International, Carnegie Museum of Art, Pittsburgh, 2008

that you're referencing, something that's been reinvented in the suburban Midlands.

RICHARD HUGHES It's almost coming through a mesh of different filters. So you work out how you're going to do something with it, and it becomes something very different and absolutely one's own as a result. When I was talking about this to my brother a while back he had an interesting take on it. He was the one into punk – the music, the clothes – but I was 10 years younger. I'd see him go out in this gear and in my head he was off to some amazing special punk place, you know, wherever these things happen. But in reality he says he was probably just walking round the corner to the park! It's those restrictions that are put on you by your circumstances, they allow those mutations to happen, and I think that kind of way of thinking has fed into a conviction to create a world of my own making.

MARTIN CLARK Your works are often made out of resin, which is a pretty blank or neutral material, a base or fundamental kind of 'stuff'. But in their finished state they have this remarkable *trompe l'oeil* quality – achieved through the casting as well as through the very painstaking way in which you paint them. I'm interested in this duality where on the one hand they have this very active, object presence, this 'thingness', but on the other hand they are all made of the same industrial material, which they kind of collapse into, and which you then paint. So as much as they are about the physical presence of the object itself, they are also about this surface you apply, they become kind of images in a way.

RICHARD HUGHES Yes, because there's never really that truthfulness to the materials. I'm presenting a very thin veneer of truth. It's about enabling me to put a stop to something, a suggestion of entropy having been frozen, so they had no chance of continuing any further, of moving towards their demise. That's total control within my means.

MARTIN CLARK It's a bit like taking a photograph.

RICHARD HUGHES I guess it is, I've never really thought about it in that way. I guess it does become more about image than object because even across the surface of these objects, I feel like something's done when my eye can go over it and not find the part that lets it down, the glitches where the making is visible. For a while I toyed with the idea of making work where the making becomes part of it in some way, the making is revealed, but I didn't think it was necessary. The work can do that without me needing to show a definite indicator of it having been made. That's what labels on walls are for. I don't mind it being quiet.

MARTIN CLARK But you're much more interested in that remove that the cast gives you, that sense of artifice, rather than bringing the actual object in? They're sculptures in a very traditional sense. It's a totally different operation, isn't it?

RICHARD HUGHES Yes, very much so, and my things could never return to the world of things, because it would be impossible for them to function, they just become stand-ins and surrogates for those things that are really out there doing their bit.

MARTIN CLARK In terms of the imagery you employ, it feels like the work inhabits a very particular sensibility, or location, it feels very autobiographical in a way. There are certain images, objects, motifs and subjects that seem very personal and that you return to again and again.

RICHARD HUGHES There are always definite objects that I return to. You know, chairs, bedding, shoes, there's a kind of sleeping quality to a lot of the work. Once a part is removed from a domestic setting and set free in the wild, it seems to punctuate that space and imply rest, or a pause somehow. The kind of places where I find the stuff I use, or suggest through their grouping in an exhibition, are far from beauty spots. Or at least they're beauty spots that are now something less, that have been tainted somehow by the activities documented by the rubbish that gathers there.

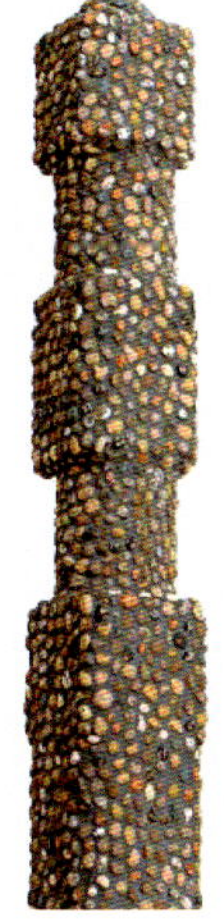

A LONG HARD STARE, 2006

MARTIN CLARK And again there's that relationship with people or bodies and what's left behind. So mattresses, sofas, clothes (*THE BIG SLEEP*, 2007), even a bottle of piss (*Roadsider (First of the Morning)*, 2005)—the sense that these things have a really strong connection to bodies that are now gone, lost, disappeared.

RICHARD HUGHES You know I never intended them to be *memento mori*, but quite often they have that feeling of time being numbered. I wouldn't say *memento mori* are necessarily a strong interest or reference for me, but they do seem increasingly relevant in relation to the work. I think a lot of the work is about time, the effect of time on me personally. I want to be able to make these pauses that focus in on small things, things that make up something bigger. That focusing in is something I've always done in the work, and as you were saying earlier, in situations when you're young, you find those moments to make your own and get lost in and inhabit for yourself. In a way I think the objects that I make are just an extension of that.

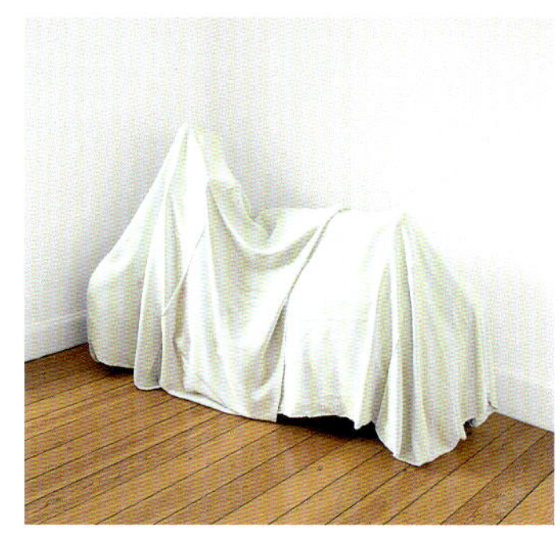

GHOST, 2011

MARTIN CLARK How do you find, or maybe select, the objects you work with? Are they things you stumble across, or are they much more deliberate? Are you hunting down things remembered, but now lost, from your own past?

RICHARD HUGHES A few years back I made a work where I cast a pair of Nike Air Pippins (*Trip Over*, 2007). It took me a while to find a pair, even with eBay, but the seed to use this specific shoe had been planted long before. I'd found a pair years earlier, in the toilets of a department store in Coventry. Someone had obviously nicked a new pair of shoes from the store and left their old ones behind. I thought they might be useful as studio footwear, so I took them, but they were just the most skanky shoes, so they stayed in the bag and got binned shortly afterwards. There was no way I was going to put my feet in them! But there was a connection with the object somehow, some potential. I kept thinking about these weird bulbous shoes, with 'AIR' stitched across them in swollen letters. The physical quality of the shoe, the really over-inflated styling and the stitch, they became really cloud-like in my mind, and that suggested a piece. Those shoes that felt like they were trying to escape, to float away or something, but they were totally anchored.

Sometimes it can be very specific, other times it can be less so. I started making a series of draped objects in 2010. Some of them were really specific, like I did a scooter, a 1960s 150 Vespa, and you could tell what it was to an extent (*Ghost*, 2011). Others were just anonymous boxes of objects (*Monday Mourning*, 2011). You don't even see what's stored. They just suggest, and were drawn from, the kinds of things stored in my studio: a box of drug paraphernalia, posters, bongs, statues, ash-trays. They were draped in the style of a Victorian funerary monument, to physically resemble that. I like this idea that garages and self-storage units round the country must be full of just these sorts of things, things that we keep because they hold the promise of re-living our youth, or implying activities we'll get back to doing one day, but which are all just left in this state of waiting. It's like waiting for the 'band gets back together' moment. There's a possibility of anthropomorphising or pareidolia, but with those objects I didn't want to go too far into that, I just let them stack, pile up, and see what's suggested.

MARTIN CLARK You've mentioned Victorian funerary monuments and *memento mori*, and for all the references to the immediate past, to the 1980s and 90s and their various subcultures, there seems to me to be something peculiarly 19th-century about your work, something almost literary. I think it's held within the operation of the objects themselves, as well as the space they create around them, but it's also there in the way that you put your shows together, the way you structure the exhibitions almost as narratives.

RICHARD HUGHES I'm aware of that myself but it's not something I intentionally pursue, possibly because I don't feel like I'm any kind of expert to comment on that or what it means historically. But I think those references just come up through familiarity, or a seed that might be planted at some moment. I've always been interested in 19th-century Romantic painting, Symbolism, Victorian art, even though I don't necessarily know how to read those codes. But no matter where these references may have come from, whatever point in history, they've all been filtered through my immediate experiences. It all comes from the catalogue of things you have around you: TV, music, film, beliefs (churches and graveyards), stories, places you visit on purpose or by accident, all the aspects of your upbringing. I'm sure that the whole idea of the magic of objects, for me, has its roots in the teachings of the Catholic Church, which was a big part of my upbringing. The acceptance that things can be transformed. Having that as part of what's in your head – believing in the power of things, the power of an object, the power of an image – before art had that affect on me, it was these ideas and images from the Church. I think I can pinpoint things in my childhood now that led to my attitude towards objects and the placing of things, that physical draping of things for instance.

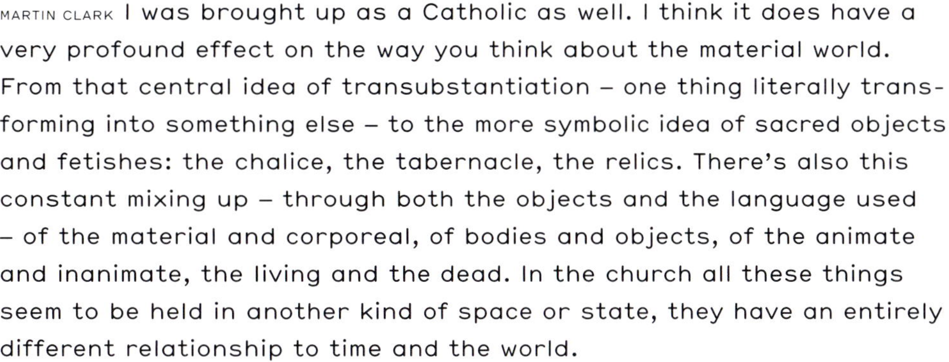

MARTIN CLARK I was brought up as a Catholic as well. I think it does have a very profound effect on the way you think about the material world. From that central idea of transubstantiation – one thing literally transforming into something else – to the more symbolic idea of sacred objects and fetishes: the chalice, the tabernacle, the relics. There's also this constant mixing up – through both the objects and the language used – of the material and corporeal, of bodies and objects, of the animate and inanimate, the living and the dead. In the church all these things seem to be held in another kind of space or state, they have an entirely different relationship to time and the world.

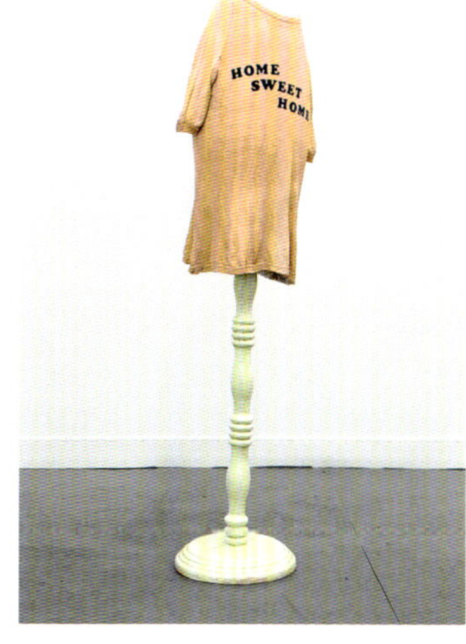

UNTITLED, 2012

RICHARD HUGHES And that stuff gets mixed up in your memories with all the other things you're discovering at that time, starting with puberty and various other awakenings. The world of things suddenly becomes a place to find your own identity, and to make some sort of decision as to how you might make your way in the world. All those things start coming together at a certain point. Looking back it was a really potent time.

MARTIN CLARK Do you feel like it's that moment that you're mining now in the work?

RICHARD HUGHES I think it is. I don't feel like I'm attempting to recreate something from that time, but I do tap into it. There are objects I'm working on now that I know go back to that moment, but at the time there was no urgency or means to do anything with it. It takes time for things to settle, and to work out which bits are poignant enough or relevant enough to bother making, really. I guess time will tell whether I'm constantly harking back to a period 20 years before what I'm working on. There's a sentimentality to time and place, I think a lot of the stuff I do is in some way holding onto that and almost dragging it out, extending the time and making it into something more real and tangible.

MARTIN CLARK In a lot of the work there's a coming together of nature and culture. I'm thinking of the sofas with funghi sprouting on them (*After the Summer of Like,* 2005), or grass growing in an old shoe (*Low Past Ya*, 2008), something being reclaimed in a way, or having an after-life now that its relationship to us is obsolete.

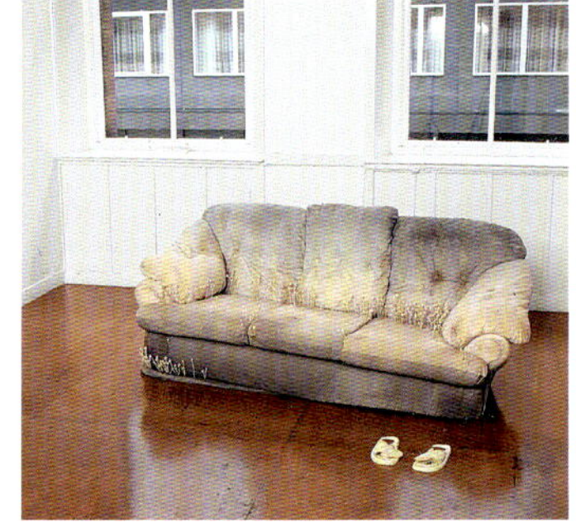

AFTER THE SUMMER OF LIKE, 2005

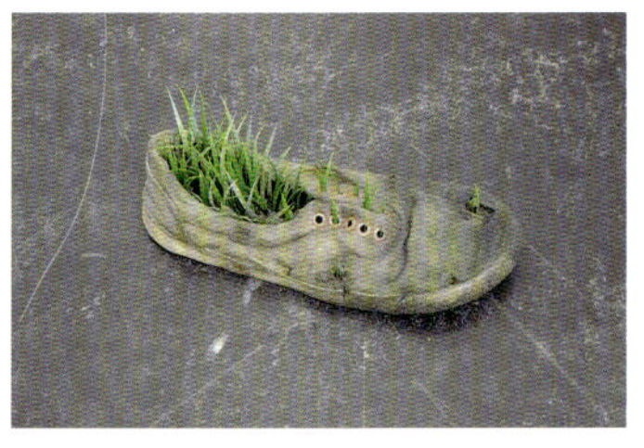

LOW PAST YA, 2008

RICHARD HUGHES I think in those works, it's almost like an elaboration of the truth. What I illustrate could just about happen, just about pass as being real. I want to push it to an illogical conclusion where it's still within the realms of reality but pushed slightly into ... I wouldn't say magic, more enchantment. But having said that, I have found real objects like that: a shoe with grass growing out of it, a mattress that's become very mossy. They're very seductive objects because they're evidence of, on a small scale, nature claiming things back, and that aesthetic appeals to me. I remember seeing a Studio Ghibli anime film on ITV one Saturday morning when I was a kid, it was called *Laputa* and it was about a city in the sky. There's this point when they reach the city up there and see these droids that are like gardeners, or maybe guardians, and I just remember seeing these robots with moss growing over them, coming out of the cracks. It was a beautiful image, gentle and quiet and haunting, it was nature claiming things back, or in conflict maybe, but in a very gentle kind of way.

MARTIN CLARK There's a great song by Silver Jews, 'The Wild Kindness', which is all about time passing, and there's a verse that goes, 'Grass grows in the ice box/The year ends in the next room/It is autumn and my camouflage is dying/instead of time there will be lateness/and let forever be delayed.' I always loved that image 'grass grows in the icebox'.

RICHARD HUGHES Something satisfyingly wrong in its rightness.

MARTIN CLARK Your works are very active, very complete and self-sufficient. As a result they seem to charge the particular space that they're in, even if they're fairly slight or discrete. They create a kind of aura.

RICHARD HUGHES It's not necessarily my works, but the initial objects that are chosen. They are, as you say, charged in some way, and I think being able to re-present them using the gallery space allows them to do that. It gives them room to give off some sort of sense of place. I think there's a strong element of landscape in my work which I'm interested in. Even if it's not landscape being represented in the object itself, it almost starts to imply the landscape that surrounds it. Your idea of what landscape or environment would surround those objects, without actually addressing the space as such.

MARTIN CLARK They do seem to produce the space around them very powerfully, they're very concentrated, potent.

RICHARD HUGHES When my girlfriend and I were living in London in 2001 and looking for our first flat, we used to look at a lot of auction places. You'd go on a Friday, pick up the keys and go into these houses that looked like the previous owners had just been wheeled out, with half their stuff still in there. More often than not it was old folk that had lived in them and their routines, their lives, were still plain to see. Most of the furniture was gone but you'd get these isolated objects still left in them, like a soap dish that had 20 years of scum, making, like, a cave; or a single drawer full of dog balls in a house that stank of dog. These things seemed to go beyond being just simple objects whose purpose had come to an end. It was something about their isolation. That specific point when almost everything had gone but there were still these few, highly charged things that were left – that residue of a life just about hanging on in there. We were just trying to find somewhere to live that we could afford, but for me personally it became a really satisfying day out, and it resolved a lot in my head, it was around that time that I began making these kinds of works.

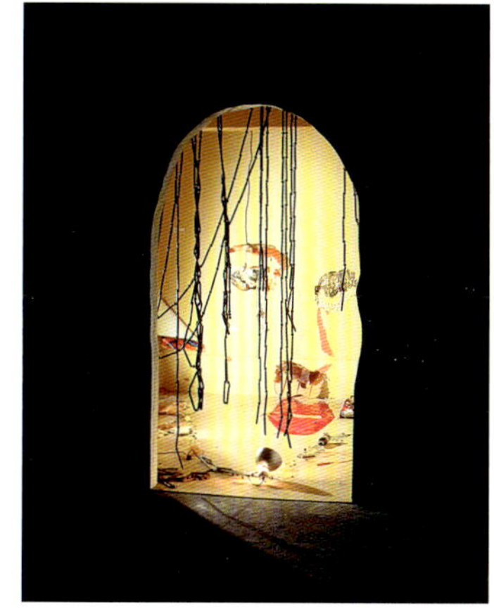

CRASH MY PARTY YOU BASTARDS, 2004

MARTIN CLARK Other works operate much more like installations, I'm thinking of a piece like *Crash My Party You Bastards*, (2004), where there's the suggestion of the aftermath of some wild party. But even in the less 'installational' works, there's often a sense of the gallery space being inhabited or occupied, squatted even. The works seem to suggest the trace of various kinds of interventions that seem more direct and sometimes more aggressive or destructive to the actual physical space itself.

RICHARD HUGHES Well they're still representations of, rather than documents of, an event. But they differ from the more stand-alone pieces in that the breakdown that you are witness to is a result of some definite activity as opposed to wear and tear. In the case of those kinds of works, the destruction that is implied is usually pretty pathetic and not particularly confrontational at all. Working more directly with a particular space is just another way to suggest more than you are presented with, a way to imply a narrative.

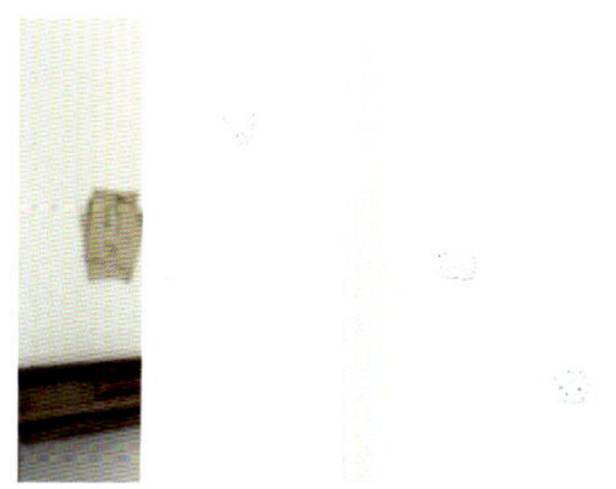

UNTITLED (SPITBALLS), 2011, DETAIL

MARTIN CLARK And are you interested in the spaces themselves, the particular context in which you've been invited to make a show? So, if it's a pristine, white cube gallery in an upscale part of a city, is it about you wanting to subvert that in some way, contaminate it even? There's that great piece with the spitballs stuck to the wall (*Untitled (Spitballs)*, 2011).

RICHARD HUGHES I think there's a slight element of that. It's like lowering the tone of the place, going back again to a grim sensibility. It's not so much an attempt at subversion, but it's more that the works need that isolation to be allowed to speak, to radiate their spores, to spread their skank and cause things to fall apart. You know, those objects, they're not quite so repulsive that you shudder—they're not gory or anything—just enough to put you off wanting to touch them! Things like the spit balls imply time again, but in a different way. Time being killed rather than just time passing. I like the sort of things that can indicate that. I have a fondness for bravado and bullying trophies: shoes hanging from overhead cables, well-aimed bike tires, underpants on a bus shelter, that sort of thing. I made a piece for The Modern Institute a few years back that blew smoke rings out of the window, it was called *Invisible Idiot* (2008). Again, it's going back to an autobiographical situation. I worked as a janitor for a while, years back, and the job involved rushing into work in the morning, getting everything done as quickly as possible, then just sitting on the roof for the rest of the day. I'm interested in that idea of killing time at a job, killing time at a bus stop ...

MARTIN CLARK Killing time in the studio as an artist ...

RICHARD HUGHES I'm eternally optimistic about time. Optimistic about being around forever in the bigger scheme of things, and on a smaller scale, optimistic about getting a piece finished for a deadline! But the reality is I'm always fighting against time and maybe that's manifesting itself via the things I make. As I get older, some of my family are growing and others are ageing and dying. Human demise becomes a real concern rather than something you just put in as a token, to signify an end in the work. There are always these stages of growth and decay within anything that's close to hand, so I do think these things to do with time and the passage of time are probably very real concerns for me now, and that's coming out more and more in the work. Or maybe I'm just becoming more conscious of it.

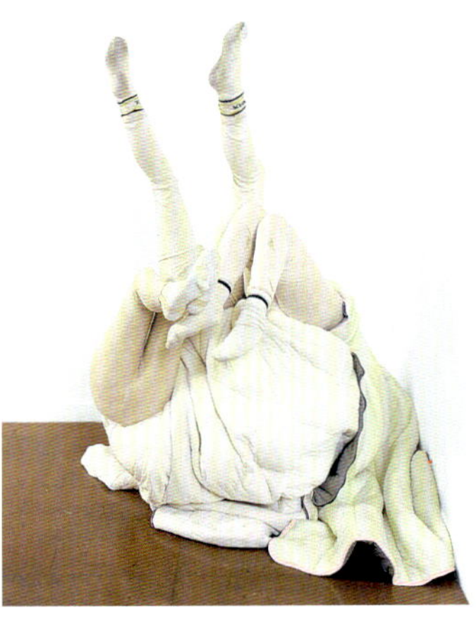

LOVE SEAT, 2005

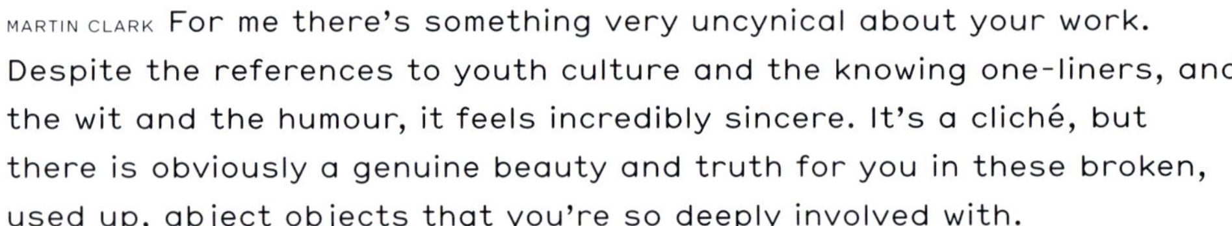

MARTIN CLARK For me there's something very uncynical about your work. Despite the references to youth culture and the knowing one-liners, and the wit and the humour, it feels incredibly sincere. It's a cliché, but there is obviously a genuine beauty and truth for you in these broken, used up, object objects that you're so deeply involved with.

RICHARD HUGHES I find comfort in them I think. Apart from the implication of a story or a history or a use, I think it's more the stillness of these things when they reach a certain point. The fact that they have been allowed to have time on their own and sit, it's that that draws me.
As a youngster I loved time-lapse photography, I was always trying to do my own, always crap. But that notion of time-lapse, of a definite period of film that might last a minute but that can potentially encapsulate months, time frozen and compressed in this film. For me, that becomes something more beautiful than the real ageing process, that simulation of time. It's not something I've ever really thought about before in terms of my own practice, but I think that in my work I'm trying to get some of the essence of that into a 'thing' rather than a film. Sometimes when I talk about my work I wonder whether what I'm trying to do and say would translate better or make more sense if I was working in another medium. But essentially that notion of bringing it back to an object is really important for me, putting all of this into a highly charged object that behaves like a relic from my own time. There's definitely something I find both poignant and comforting in objects that have reached that stage, a redemptive quality where the mask of shit slips to reveal a glimpse of the sublime.

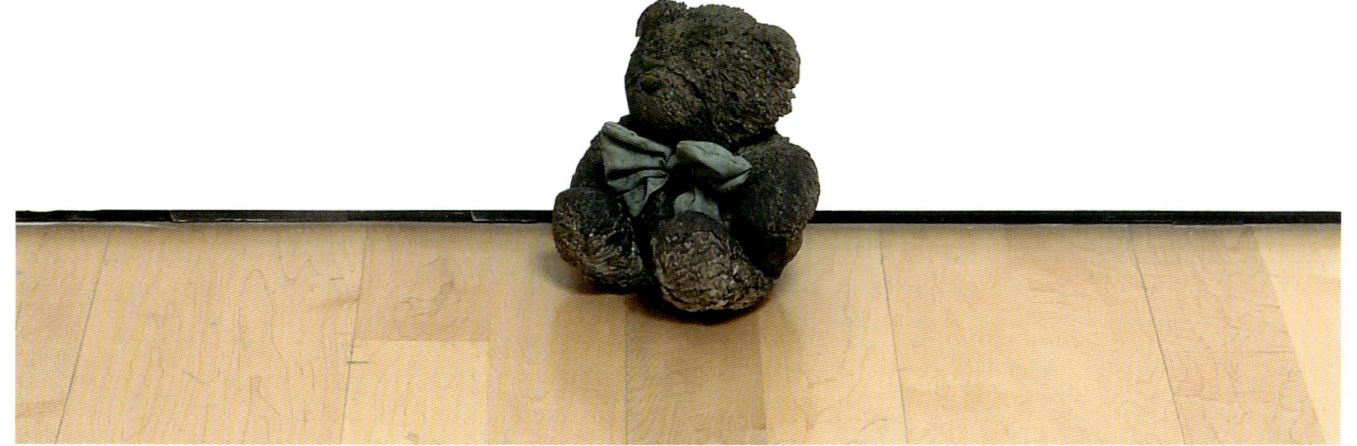

TOO LONG AT THE FAIR, 2008

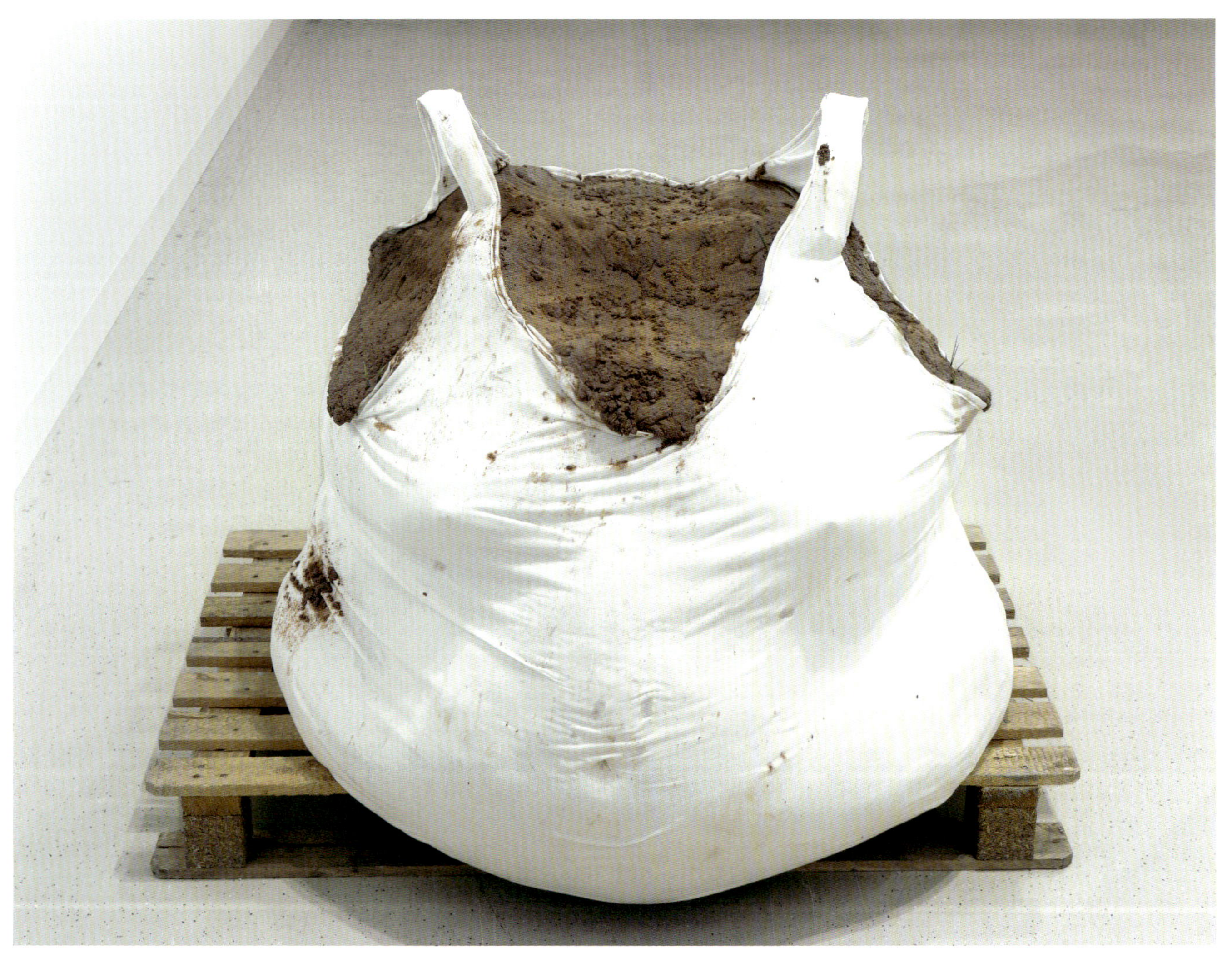

POETS DAY, 2009

TOWER OF HEADS, 2011

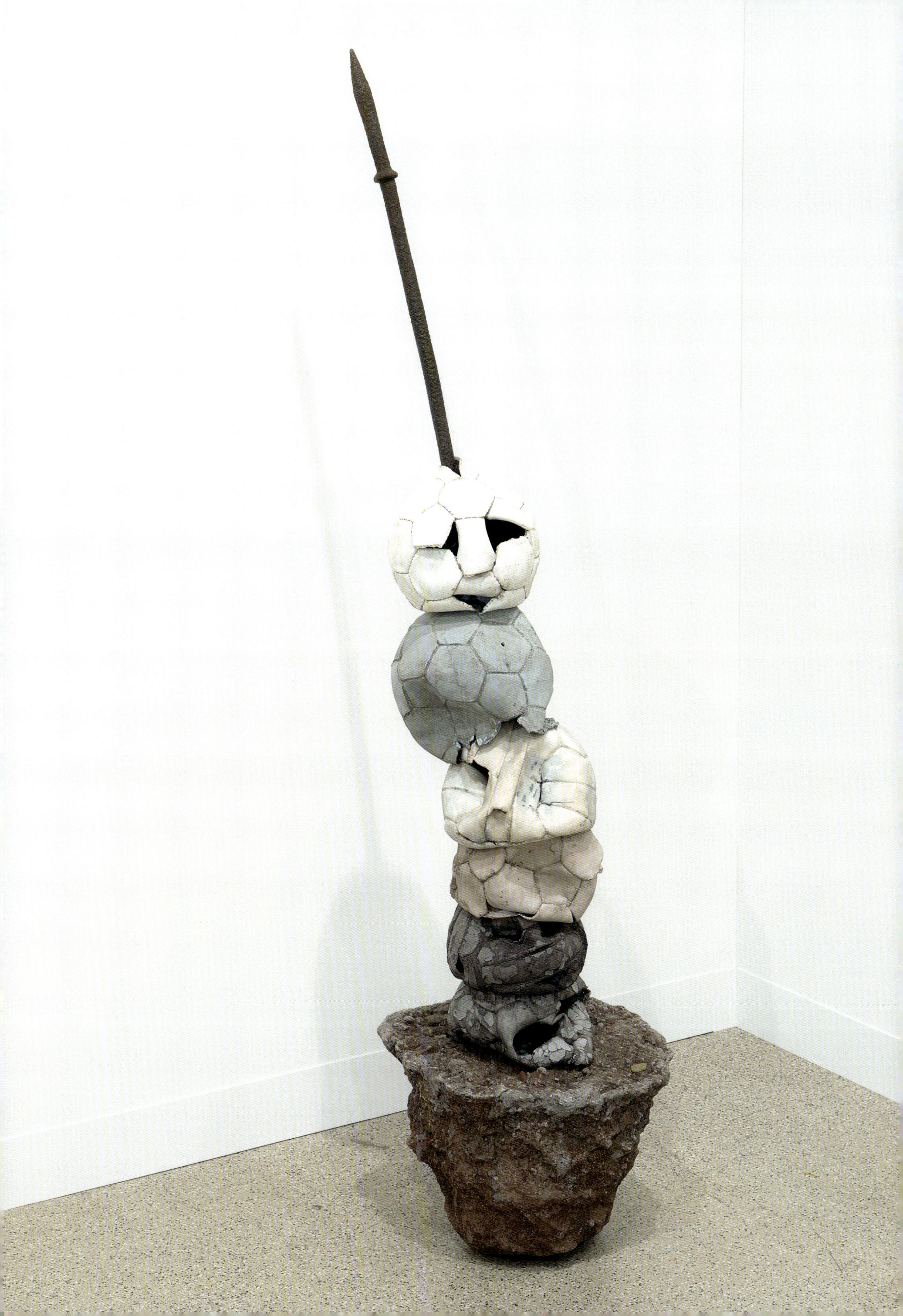

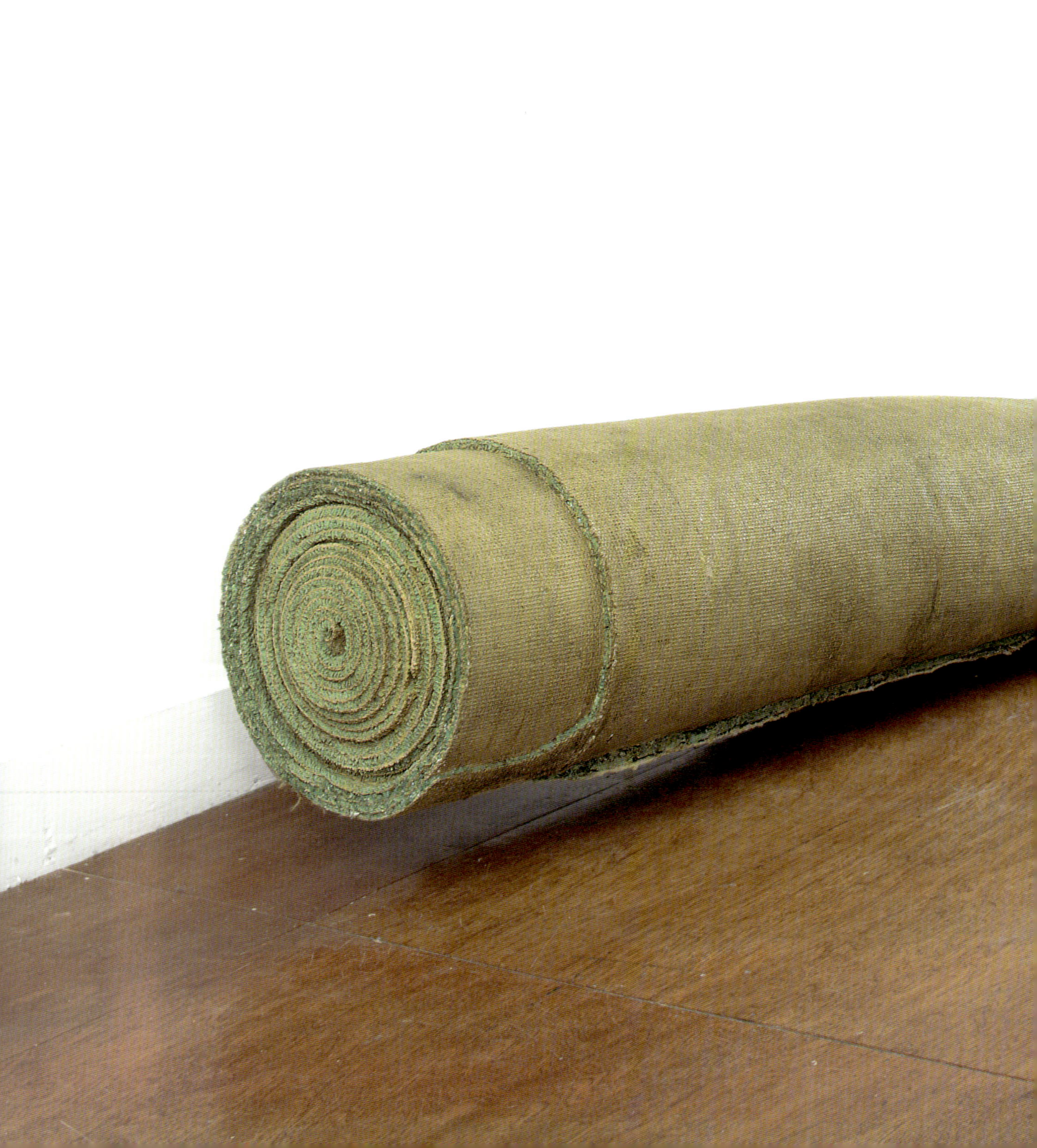

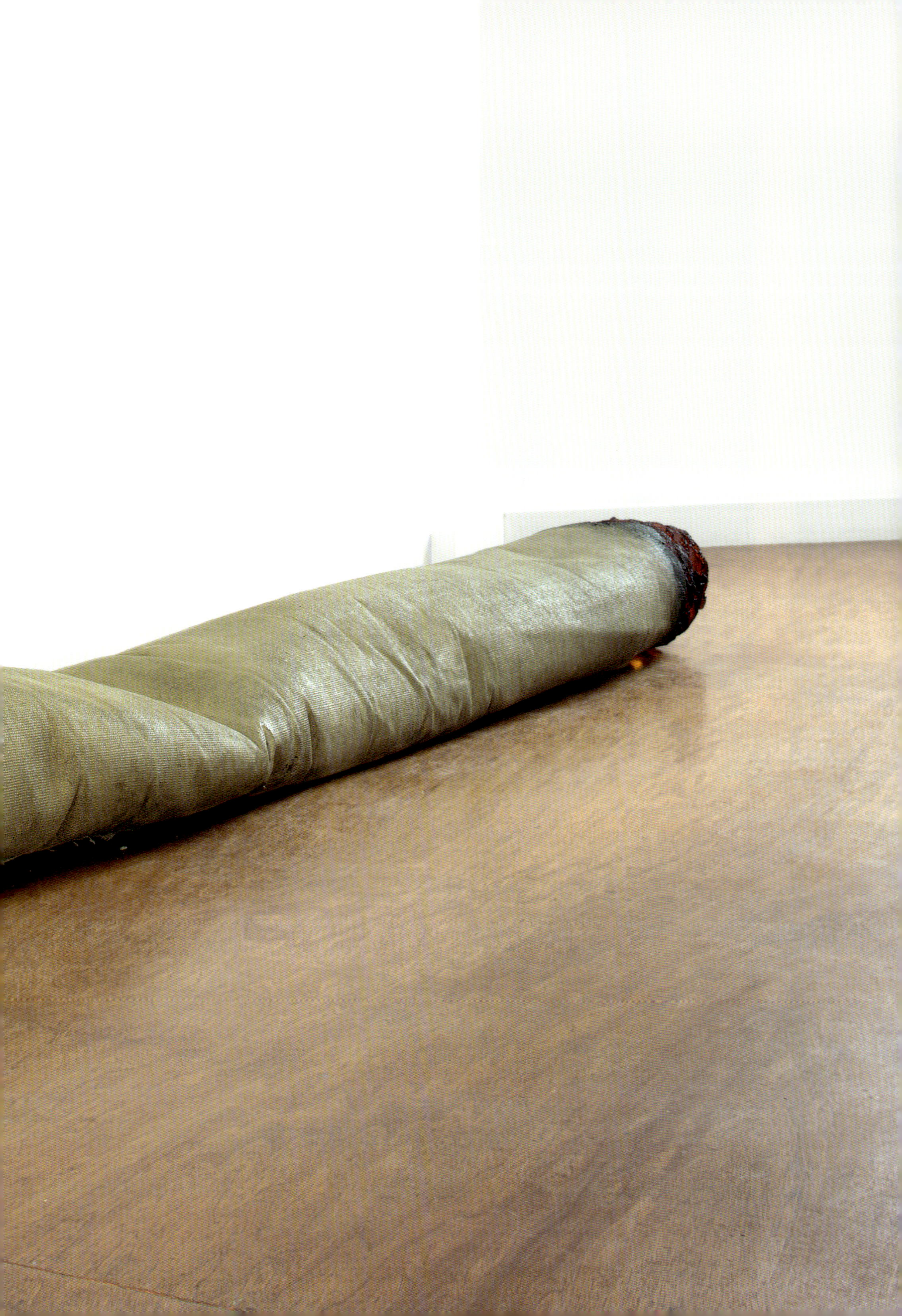

SUPERKING, 2008

←

BROKEN CIRCLE, 2006, detail

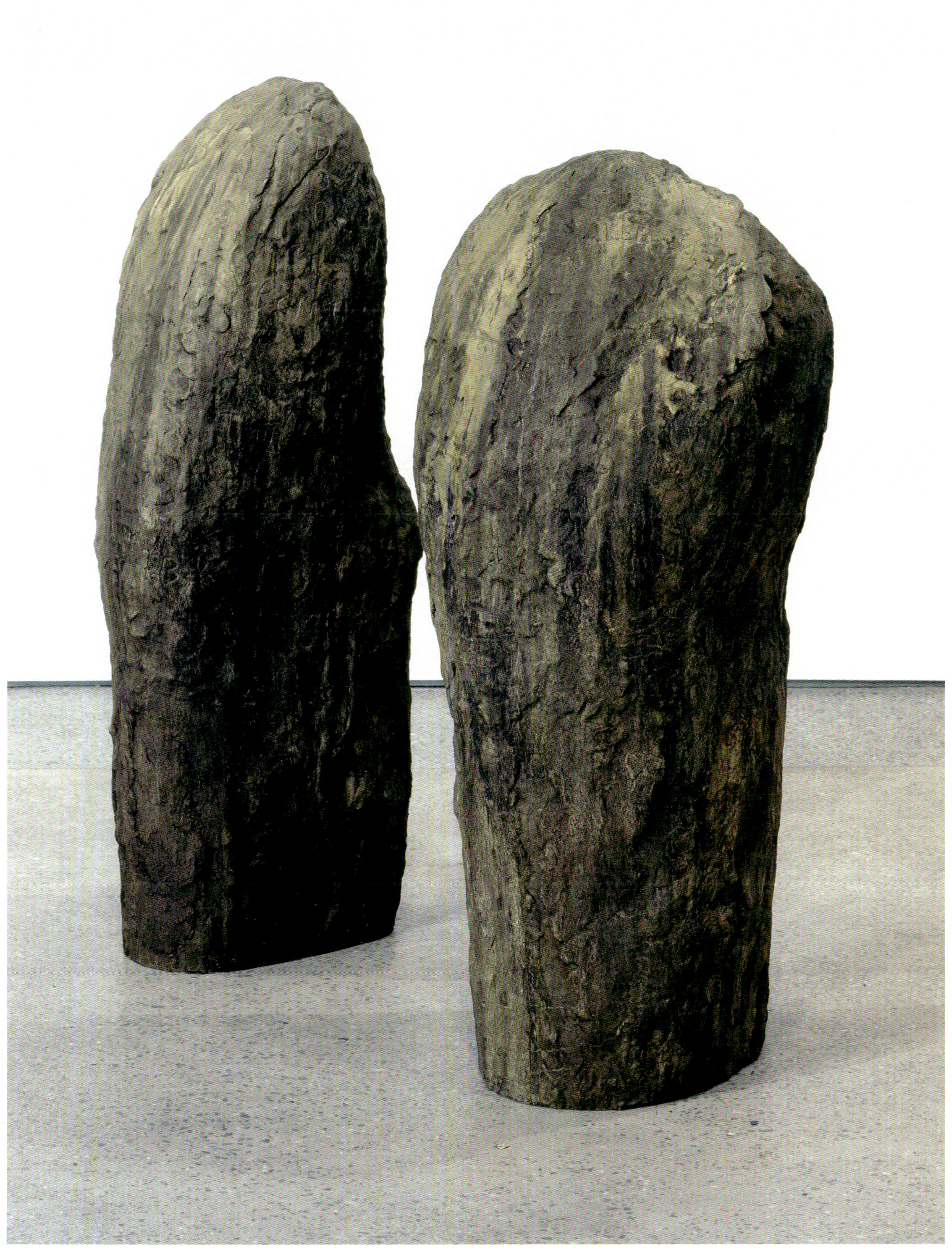

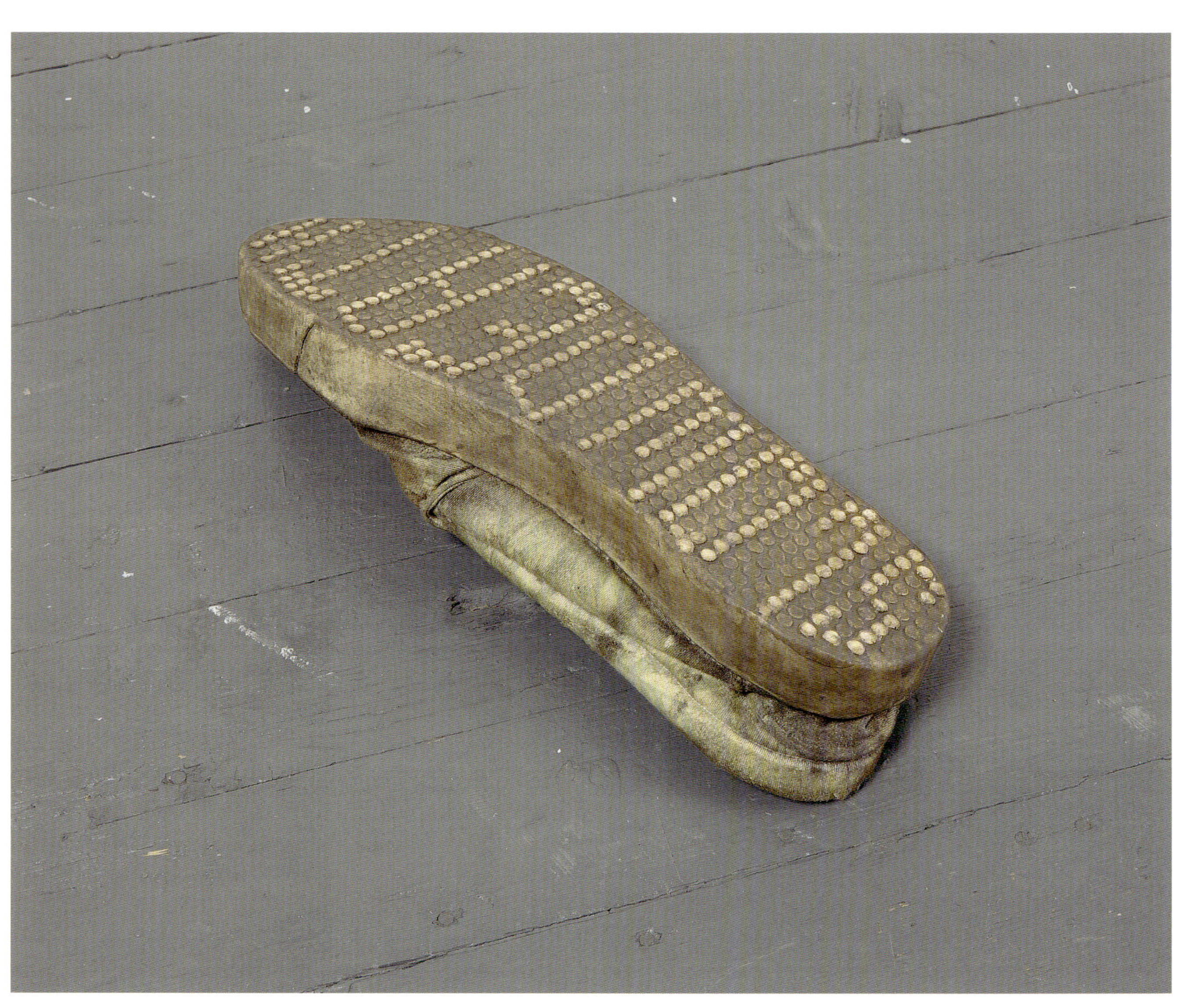

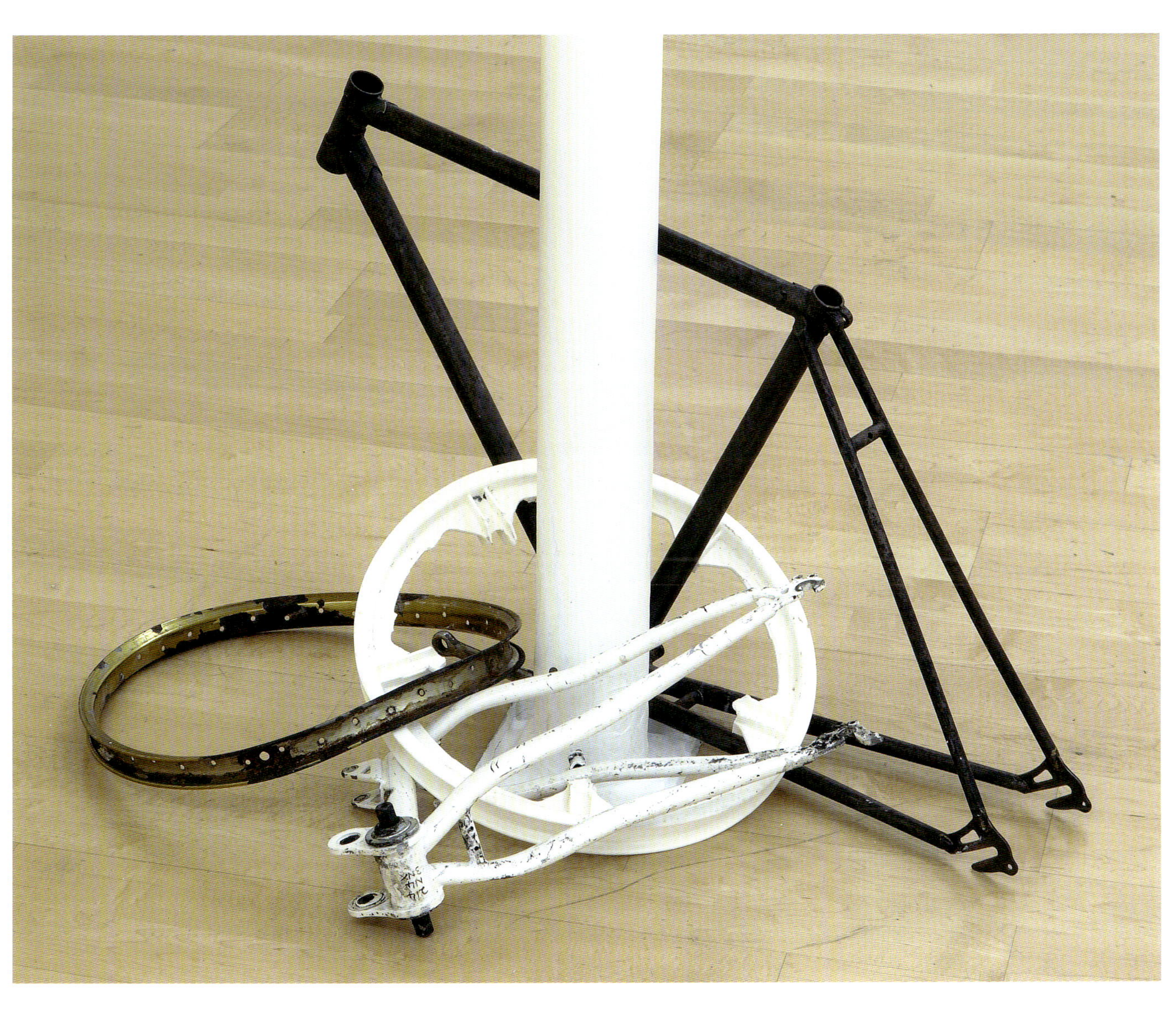

TRIPTICK, 2011

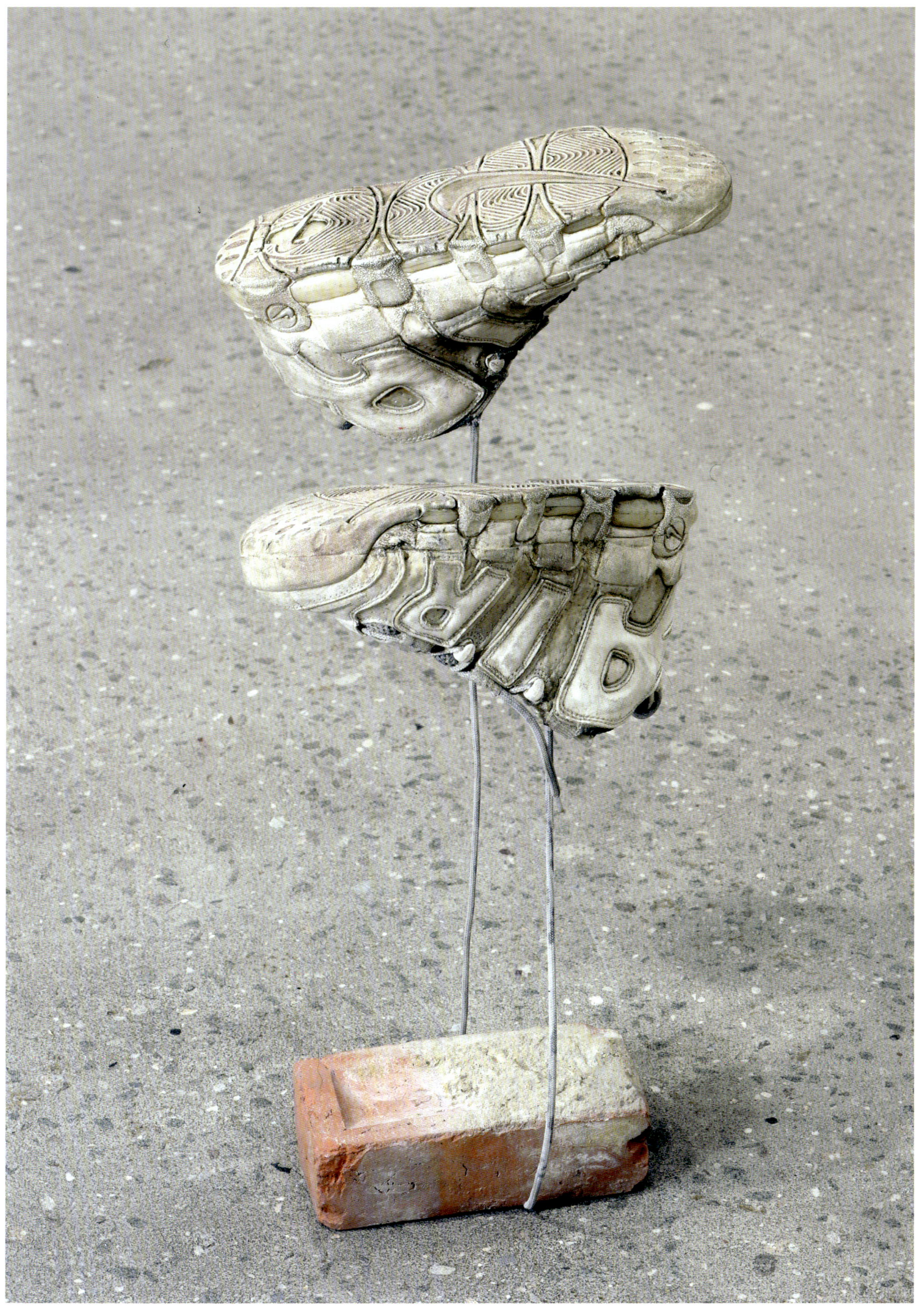

TRIP OVER, 2007

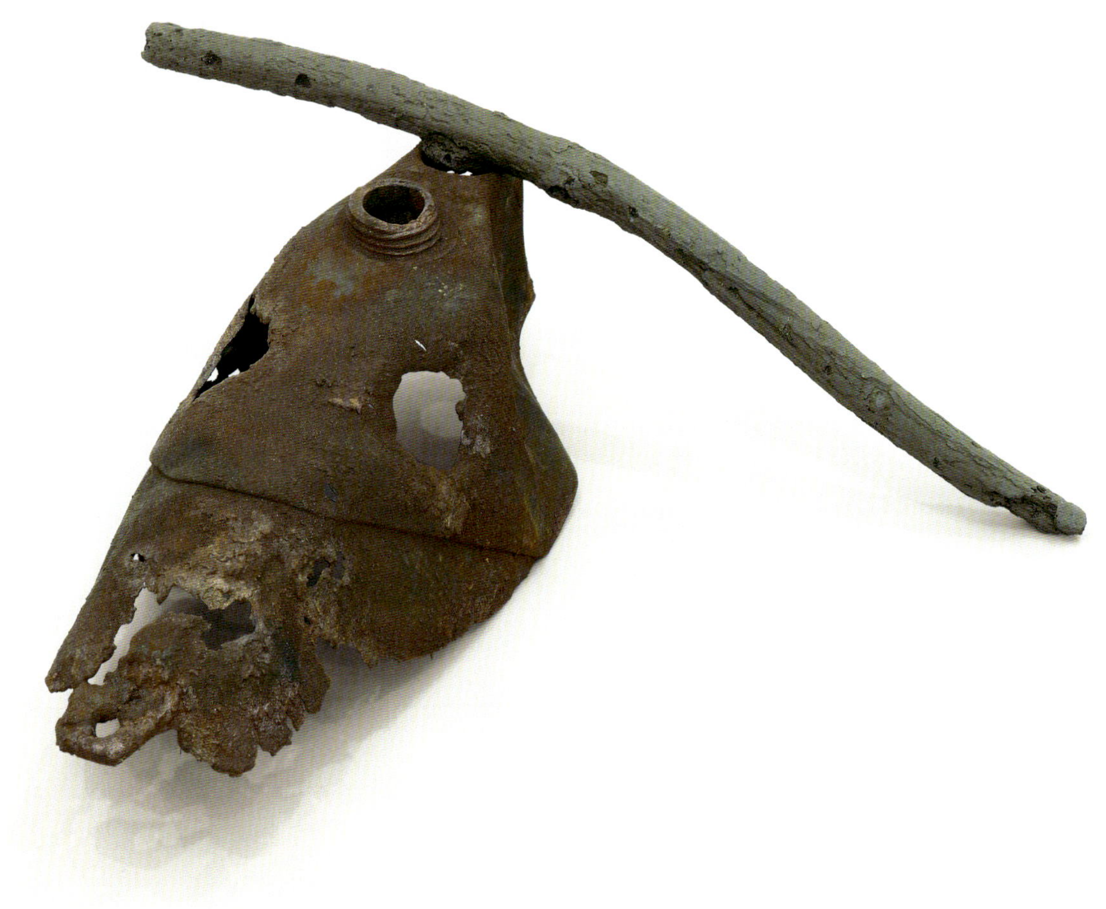

LANDFILL, 2010

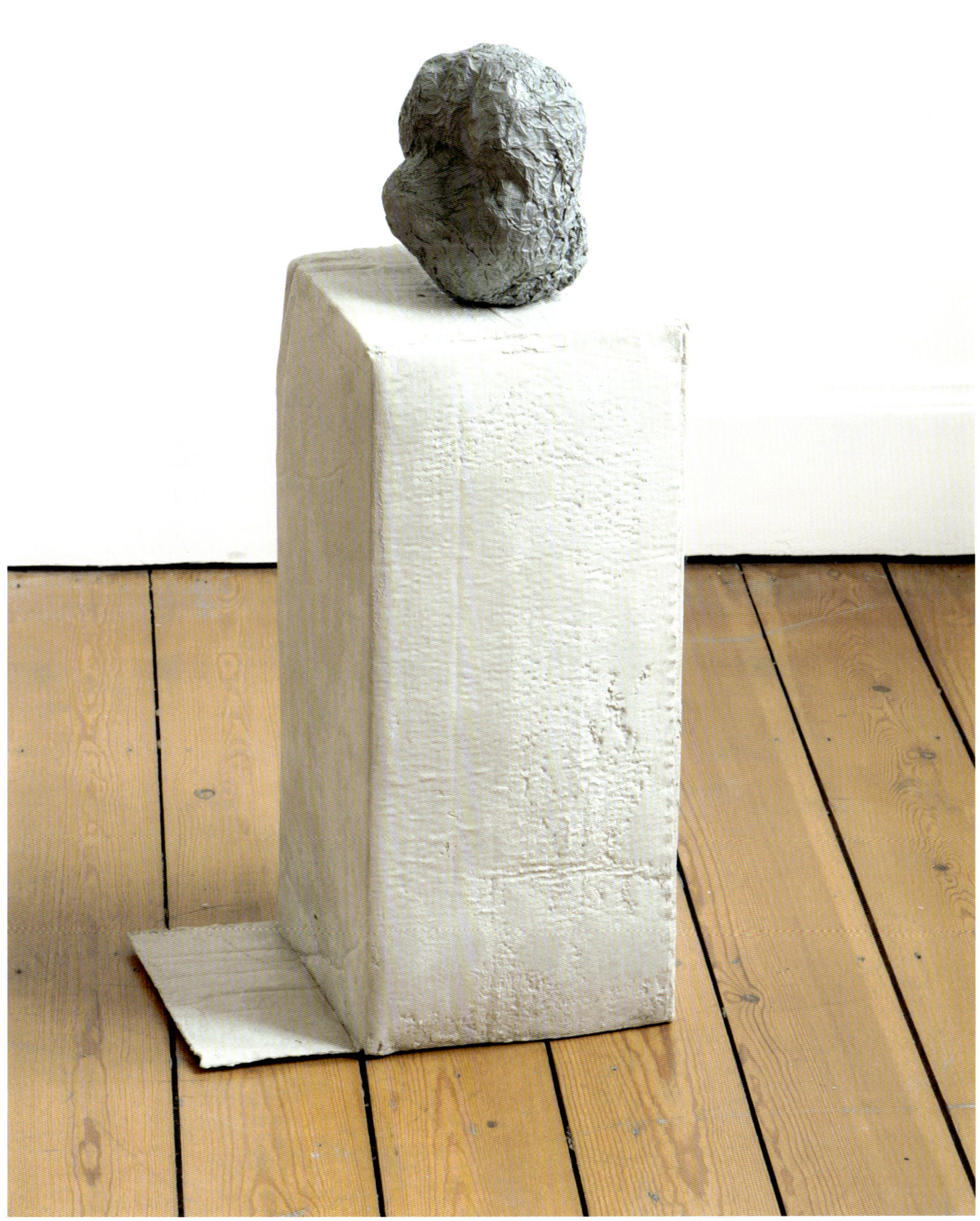

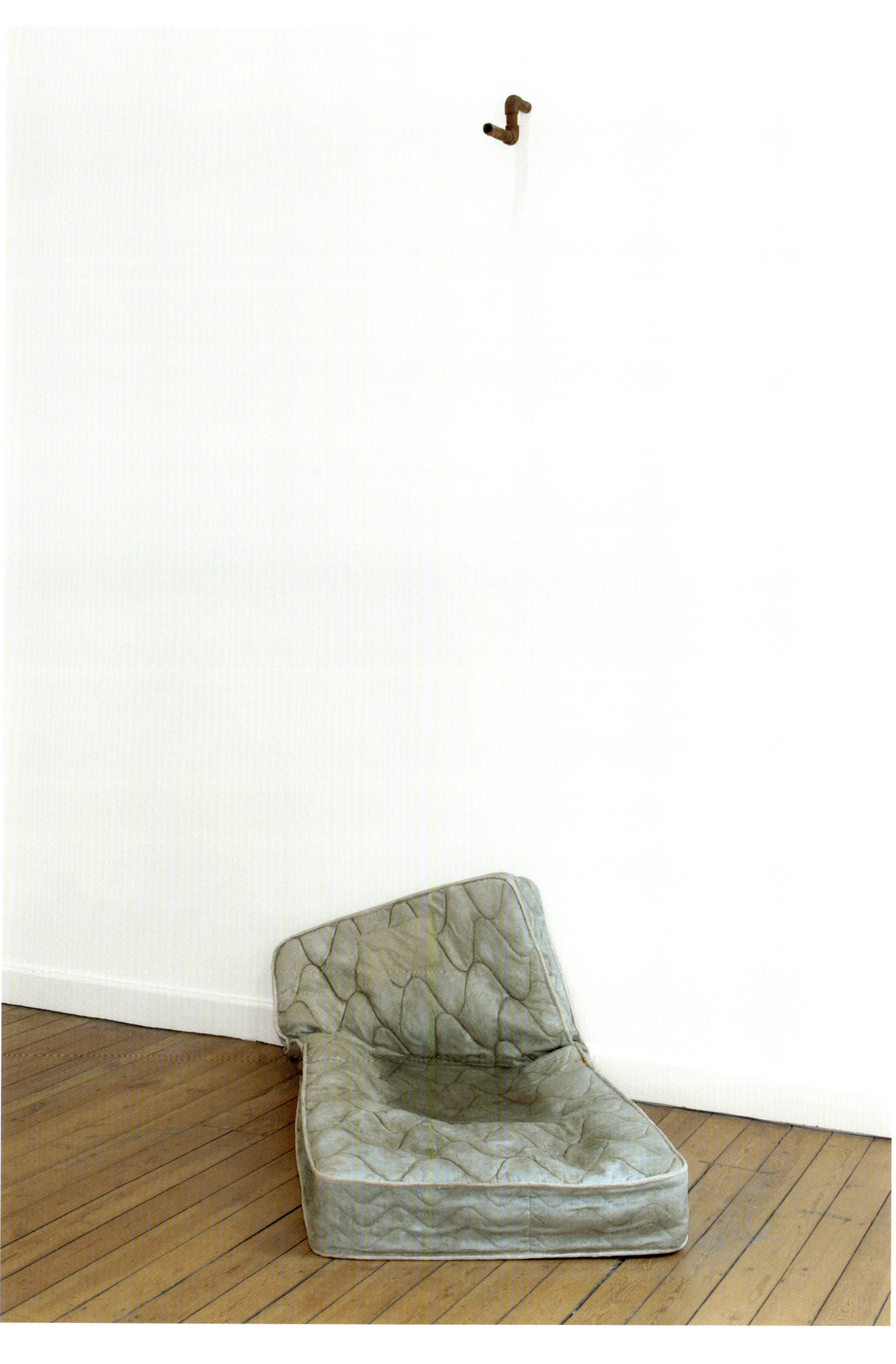

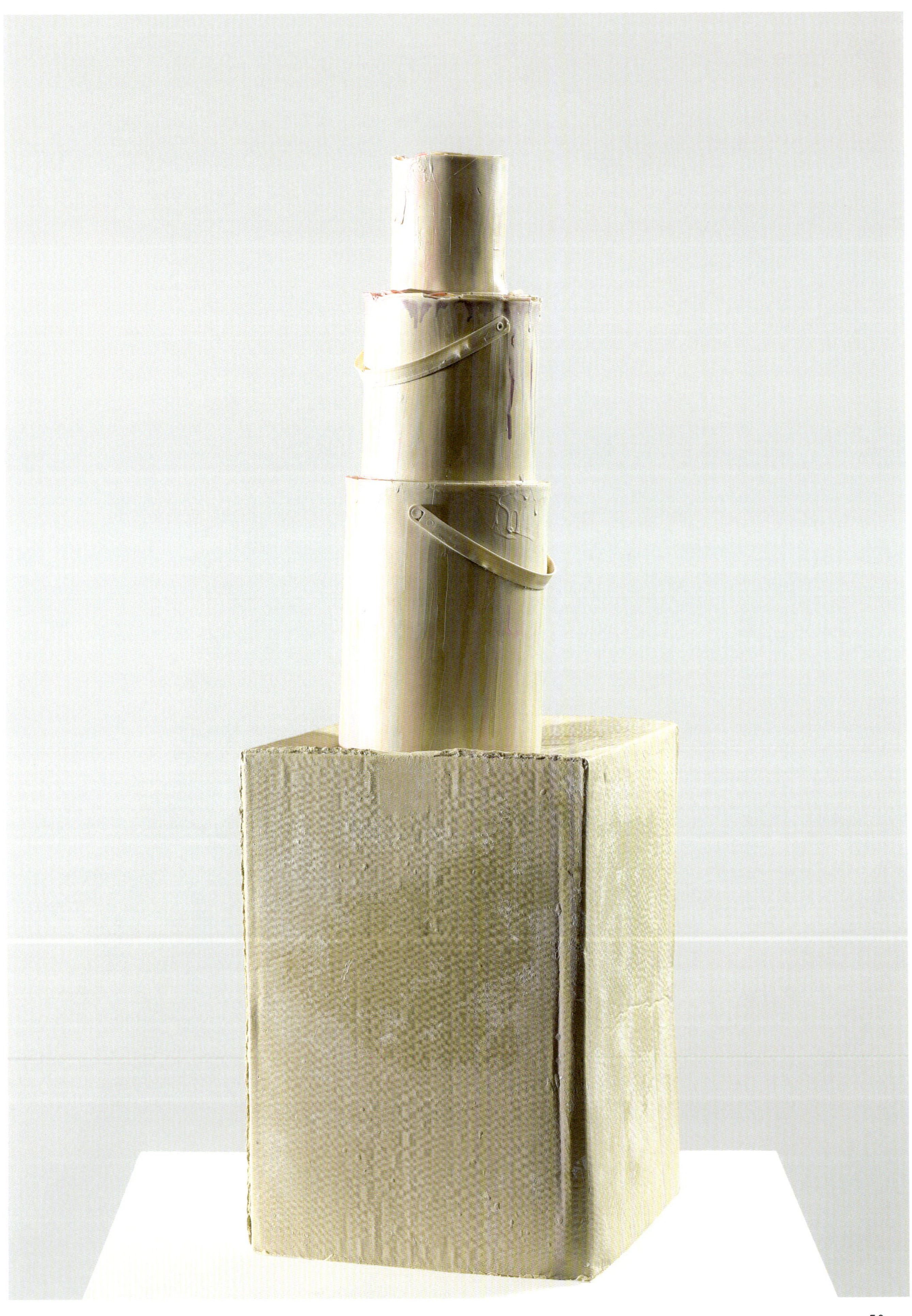

WASHOUT, 2006

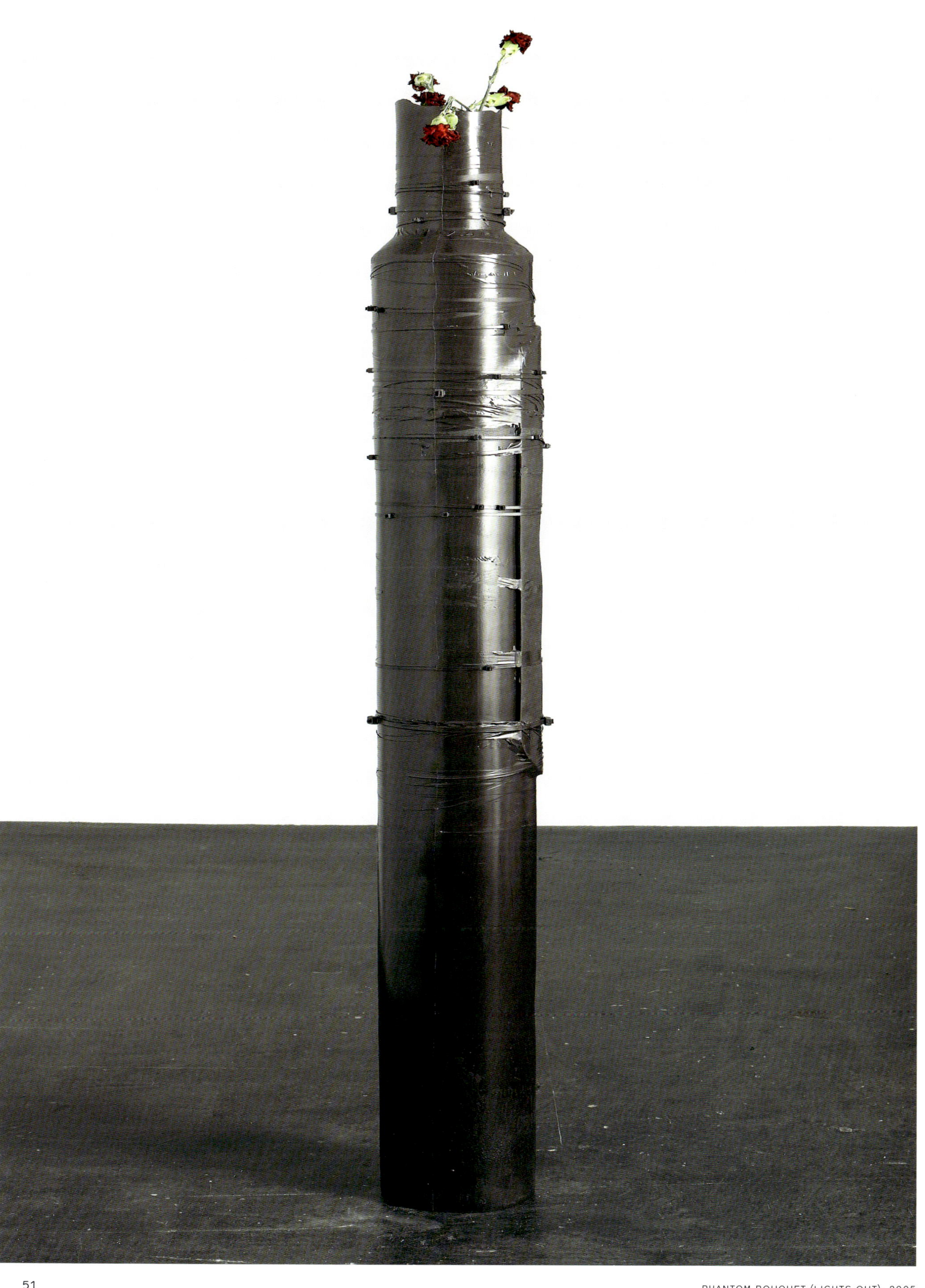

PHANTOM BOUQUET (LIGHTS OUT), 2005

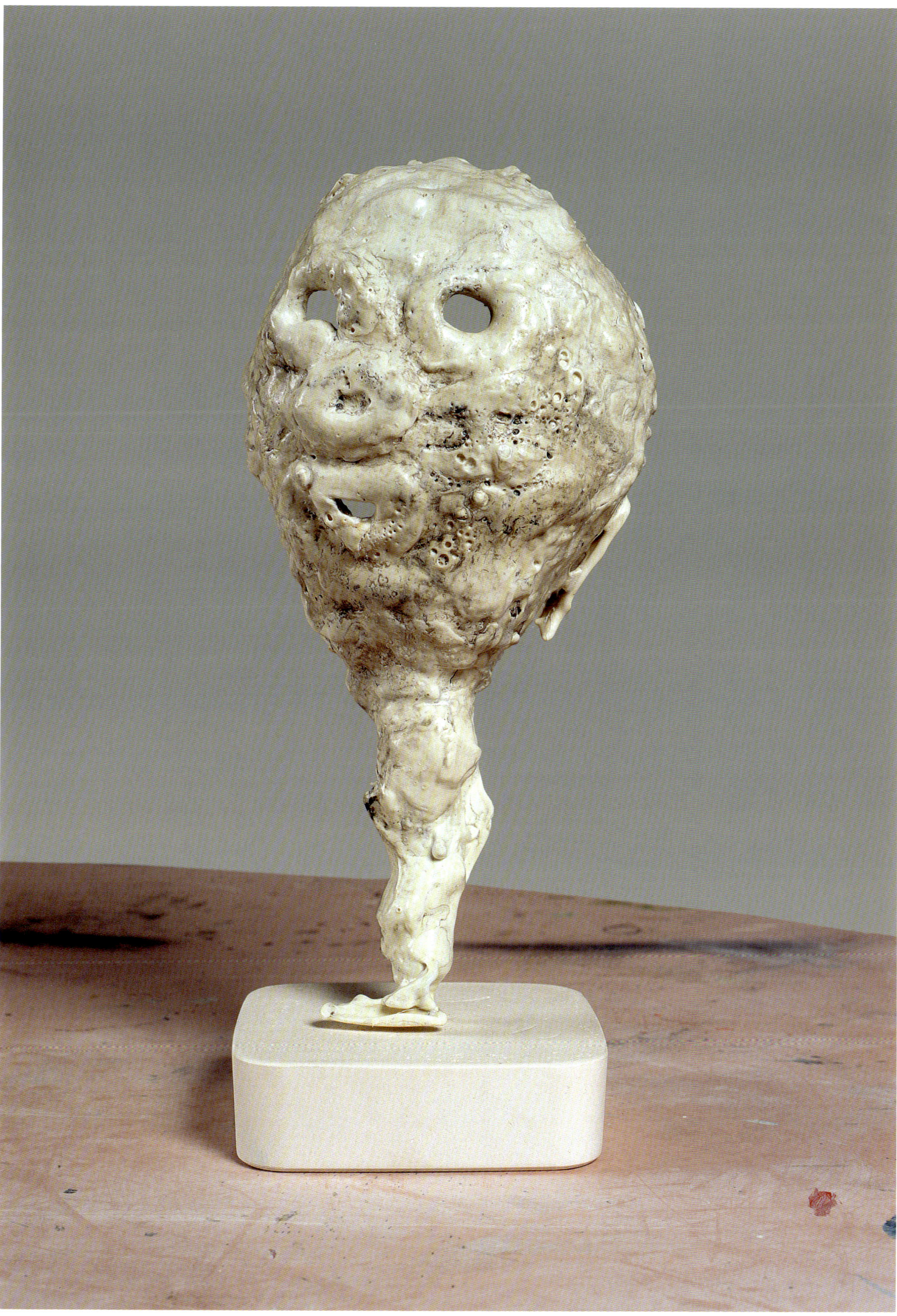

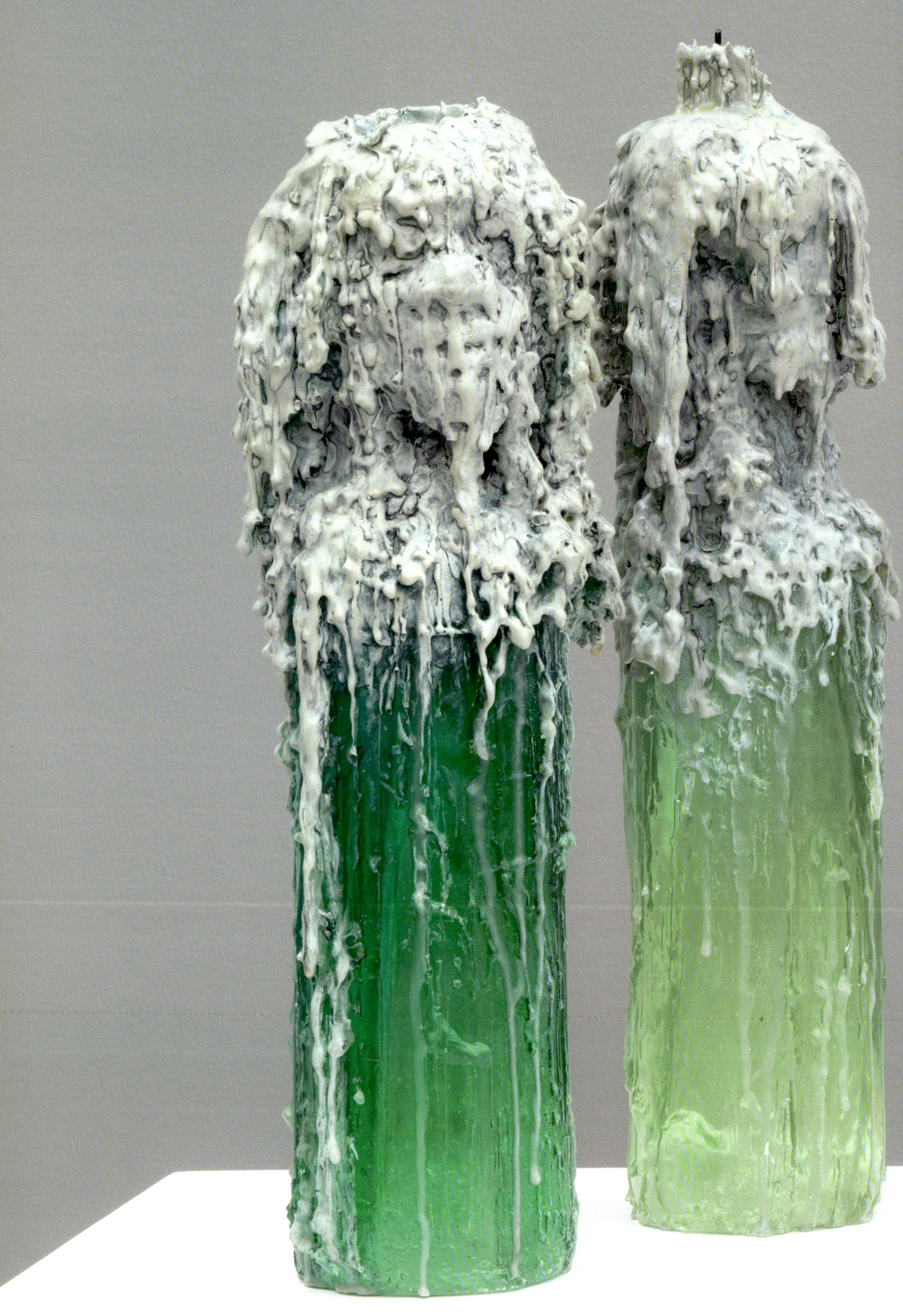

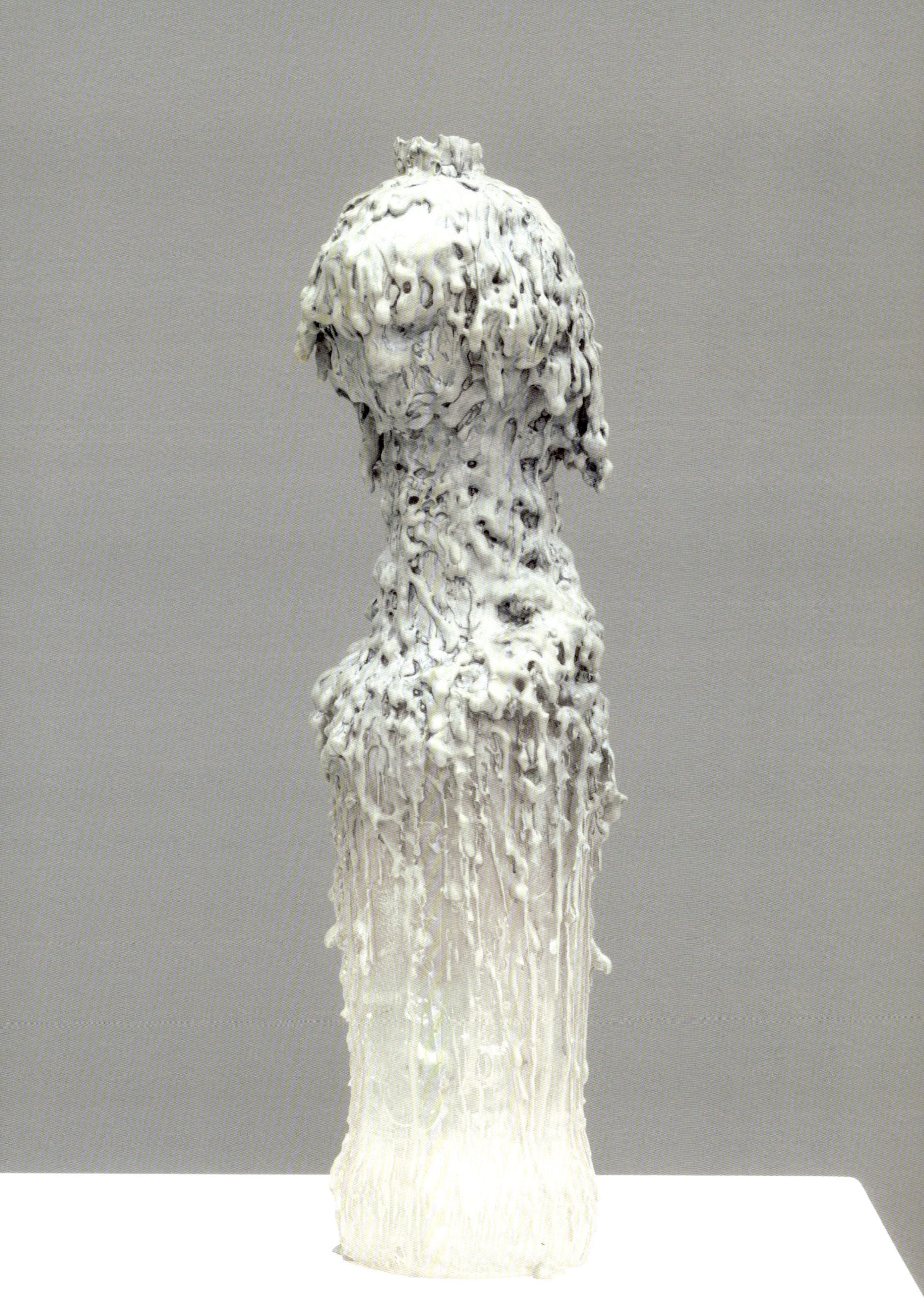

ALNIGHT ROW, 2011

←

GRIMEWAVE, 2011

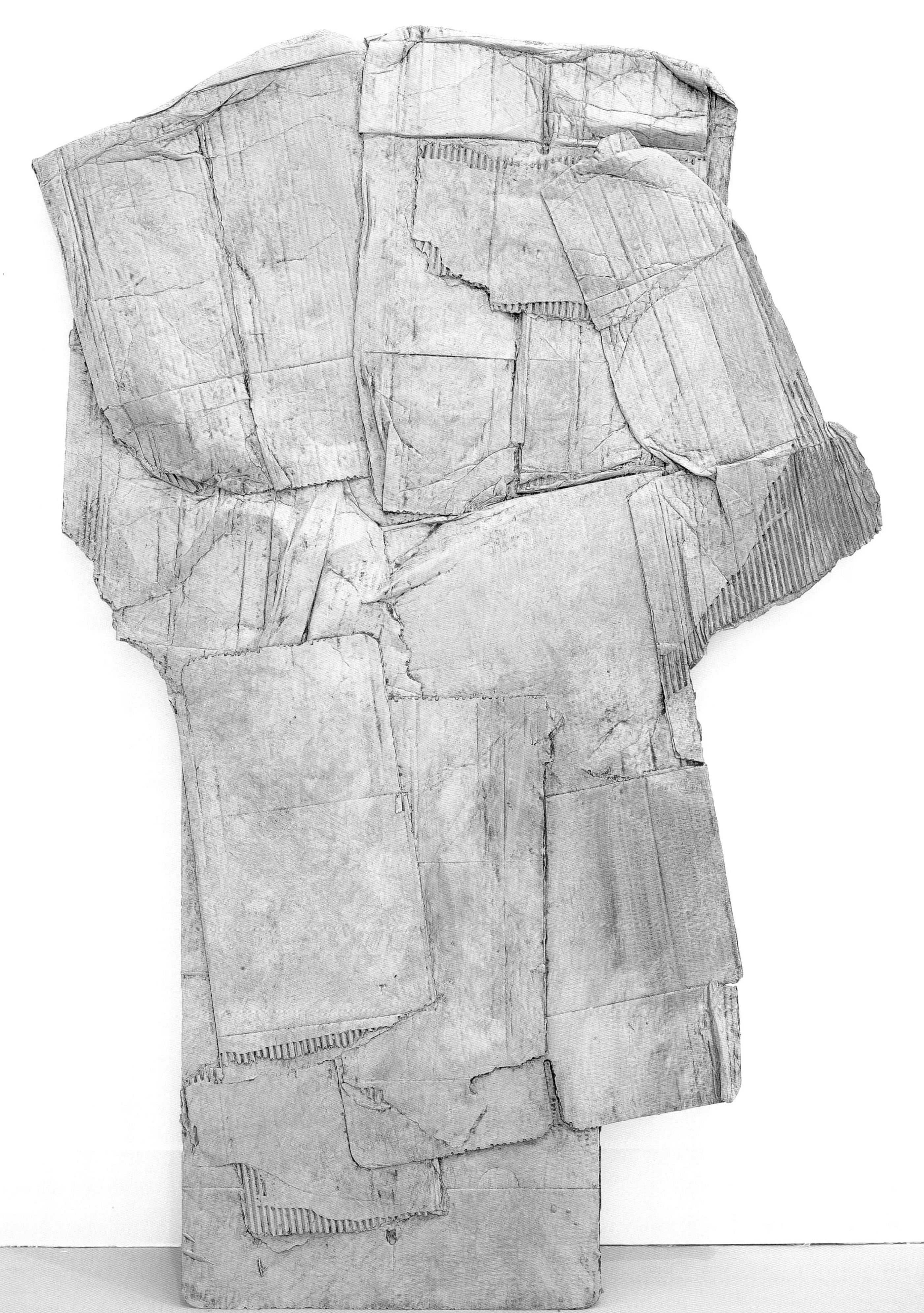

PRISON TATTOO (2), 2011

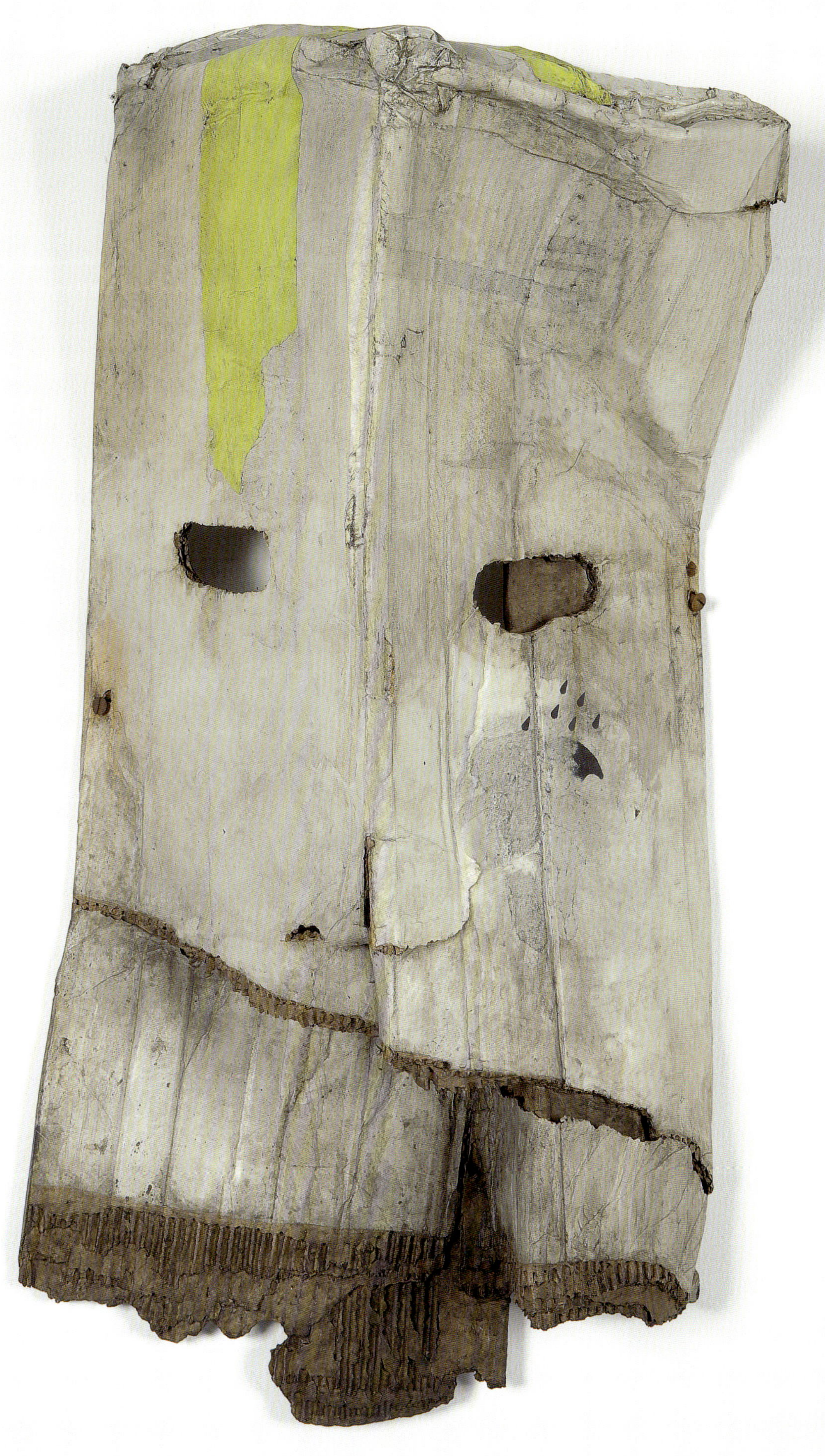

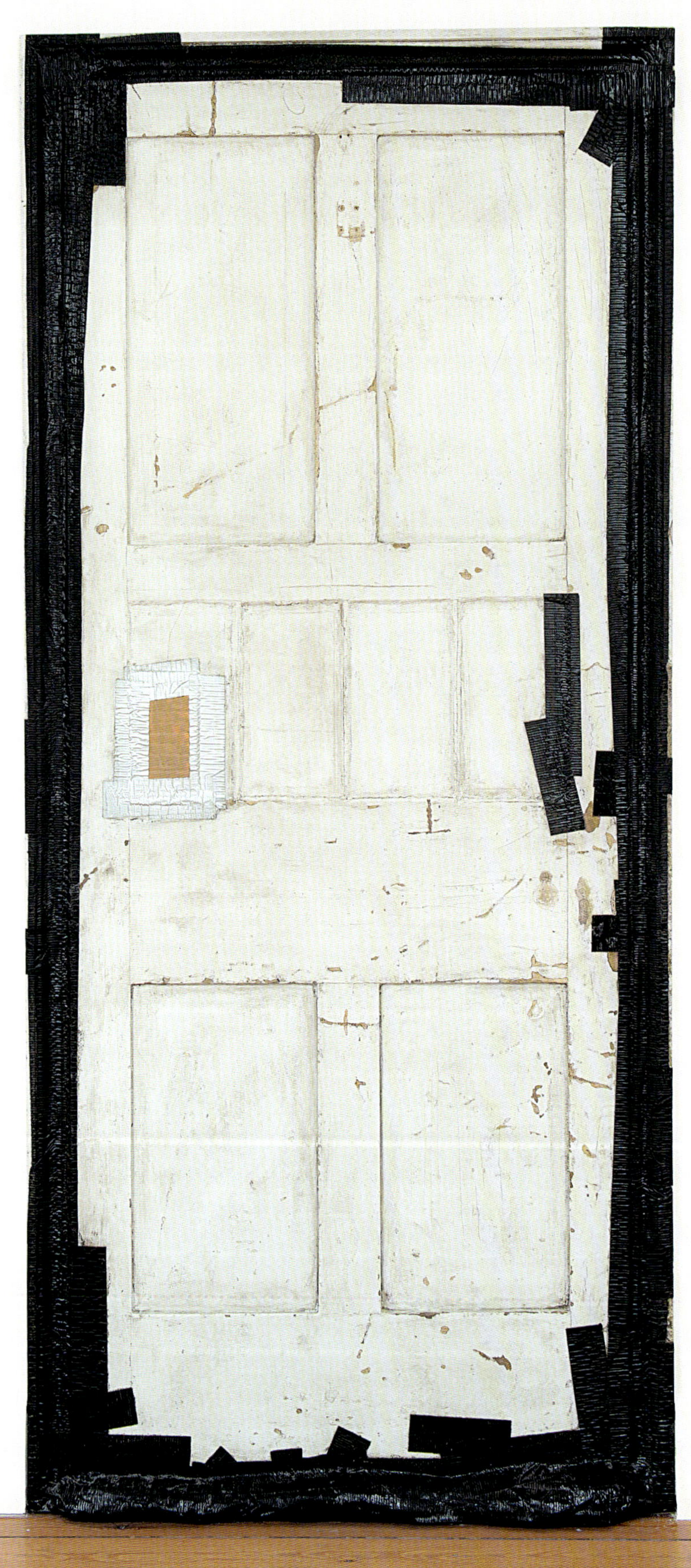

GAP FILLER, 2011

Biographies

1974
Born in Birmingham (UK), Richard Hughes lives and works in Herefordshire
2003
Graduated from Goldsmiths, University of London

SOLO EXHIBITIONS (SELECTION)
2012
Where It All Happened Once, Tramway, Glasgow
2011
Endless Bummer, Barbara Gladstone Gallery, Brussels
2010
Richard Hughes, Anton Kern Gallery, New York
2008
nothing left, it's alright, The Modern Institute, Glasgow
One Man's Struggle To Take It Easy, Sadie Coles HQ, London
2007
Richard Hughes, Anton Kern Gallery, New York
2006
Richard Hughes: Keep On Onnin', Art Now, Sculpture Court, Tate Britain, London
2005
Richard Hughes, The Modern Institute, Glasgow
What A Dude'll Do, Nils Staerk Contemporary Art, Copenhagen
2004
Richard Hughes, Roma Roma Roma, Rome
The Shelf-life of Milk, The Showroom, London

GROUP EXHIBITIONS (SELECTION)
2012
Undervæker–Mesterværker Fra Danske Privatsamlinger, Kunsten Museum of Modern Art, Aalborg
2011
Yes, We Don't, Institut d'art contemporain, Villeurbanne
2010
Rive Gauche, Rive Droite, Marc Jancou Contemporary, Paris*
Country Music, Blum and Poe Gallery, Los Angeles
2009
TONITE, The Modern Institute, Glasgow
Mapping the Studio, Palazzo Grassi, Venice
Suns Neither Rise Nor Set, Royal College of Art, London
2008
All Inclusive. A Tourist World, Schirn Kunsthalle, Frankfurt
Des Hughes and Richard Hughes, Michael Benevento, Los Angeles
Life on Mars–55th Carnegie International, Carnegie Museum of Art, Pittsburgh
2007
Re-dis-play, Kunstverein Heidelberg, Heidelberg
The Zabludowicz Collection, Baltic Centre for Contemporary Art, Gateshead
2005
British Art Show 6, Baltic Centre for Contemporary Art, Gateshead
The Pantagruel Syndrome, The Turin Triennial, Turin

Joanne Tatham is an artist who usually works in collaboration with Tom O'Sullivan.
Martin Clark is Artistic Director at Tate St Ives.

* Publication

List of Works Reproduced

Cover
Deepending, 2006, detail
Chair, dye, fibreglass, wire, modelling putty, enamel, resin, 51 × 69 × 86 cm
James Moores Collection, Gloucestershire

Endpapers
You Had to Be There, 2006
Digital C-type print, 61 × 48 cm, edition of 3
Jud Laird Collection, Miami Beach

[p. 1] *Mask*, 2011
Polyester resin cast, fibreglass, 44 × 48 × 2 cm
[p. 2] *Diamond Dust*, 2010
Jesmonite, GRP, polyester resin, paint, electric lights, 193 × 152 × 30.5 cm
[p. 5] *Shut Down 2*, 2010
Fiberglass, polyester resin, iron powder, acrylic paint, 241 × 244 cm
Cohen Collection, New York
[p. 7] *Shut Down 1*, 2010
Fiberglass, polyester resin, iron powder, acrylic paint, 244 × 93 cm
[p. 8] *The Legendary Chock*, 2007
Cast silicone rubber, stitched canvas, cast concrete, cast polyurethane, acrylic paint, 39 × 283 × 22 cm
Jill & Peter Kraus Collection, New York
[p. 9] *THE BIG SLEEP*, 2007
Jesmonite, pigment, acrylic paint, modeling putty, plastic, 24 × 191 × 91 cm
Ovitz Family Collection, Los Angeles
[p. 11] *The Malingerer*, 2010, detail
Fiberglass, polyester resin, polyurethane resin, iron powder, 335 × 67 cm
[p. 12–13] Installation view, Anton Kern Gallery, New York, 2010
[p. 14–15] *Jimmy, Jimmy (The End)*, 2010, detail
Clay tiles, plaster board, paper, wood, paint, vinyl tiles, carpet, cork, 672 × 495 × 28 cm
Richard Prince Collection, New York
[p. 17] *Deepending*, 2006
Chair, dye, fiberglass, wire, modeling putty, enamel, resin, 51 × 69 × 86 cm
James Moores Collection, Gloucestershire
[p. 18–19] *we're all mad*, 2008
Polyester resin, jesmonite, modeling putty, wire, acrylic paint, dirt, 135 × 41 × 43 cm
Ovitz Family Collection, Los Angeles
[p. 20] *Ghost Paw*, 2006
Epoxy resin, metal rods, jesmonite, dried leaves, enamel, acrylic paint, 34 × 25 × 13 cm
[p. 21] *It is Never Too Late To Become What You Might Have Been*, 2008, detail
Bronze, 480 × 230 × 210 cm
[p. 22] *Untitled*, 2007
Polyester resin, fiberglass, epoxy, putty, steel wire, enamel, acrylic paint, varnish, 140 × 80 cm
Private Collection, London
[p. 23, 24] *Wot we did on our holidays*, 2010
Polyester, resin, fiberglass, jesmonite, enamel, electric lights, 50 × 220 × 40 cm
[p. 26] *Small Town Big Man*, 2011
Acrylic and enamel paint on GRP, 110 × 51 × 25 cm
Mark Fletcher and Tobias Meyer Collection, New York
[p. 27] *Monday Mourning*, 2011
Cast polyester, polyurethane resin, phosphorescent pigment, acrylic paint, enamel, 87 × 75 × 55 cm
Pamela and Arthur Sanders Collection, Greenwich, CT
[p. 28] Installation view, *Life on Mars*, 55th Carnegie International, Carnegie Museum of Art, Pittsburgh, 2008
[p. 29] *A Long Hard Stare*, 2006
MDF, polymer clay, jesmonite, grout, 230 × 11 × 11 cm
Rosetta Delug Collection, Beverly Hills, CA

[p. 30] *Ghost*, 2011
Polyester resin cast, fiberglass, 105 × 166 × 66 cm
[p. 31] *Untitled*, 2012
Cast polyester resin, fiberglass, enamel, acrylic paint, 175 × 40 × 38 cm
[p. 32] *After the Summer of Like*, 2005
Re-upholstered sofa, hand-dyed canvas, wire, modeling putty, spray paint, enamel, 82 × 204 × 89 cm
Speyer Family Collection, New York
Low Past Ya, 2008
Cast polyurethane resin, stitched and dyed canvas, metal eyelets, laces, modeling putty, wire, acrylic paint, plastic, 32 × 12 × 13 cm
Eugene Sadovoy Collection, Los Angeles
[p. 33] *Crash My Party You Bastards*, 2004
Mixed media, dimensions variable
Private Collection
Untitled (Spitballs), 2011, detail
Painted bronze, 56 spitballs, dimensions variable
[p. 34] *Love Seat*, 2005
Fiberglass, polyurethane foam, dyed clothing, bedding, 188 × 87 × 86 cm
Private Collection, Paris
[p. 35] *Too Long at the Fair*, 2008
Polyester resin, paint, 22 × 22 × 12 cm
Private Collection
[p. 36] *Poets Day*, 2009
Fiberglass, fabric, pallet, 100 × 110 × 105 cm
Ludivine & Gregory Touret Collection, Paris
[p. 37] *Tower of Heads*, 2011
GRP, cast polyurethane, enamel, iron powder, acrylic paint, 170 × 42 × 37 cm
Ole Faarup Collection, Copenhagen
[p. 38–39] *Superking*, 2008
Fiberglass, polyester resin, polyurethane, enamel, acrylic, electric lights, 292 × 30 × 34 cm
Giancarlo and Sandra Bonollo Collection, Vicenza
[p. 41] *Broken Circle*, 2006, detail
Polystyrene, wire, jesmonite, stone powder, epoxy resin, leaves, lacquer, acrylic paint; three parts, part 1: 170 × 80 × 80 cm, part 2: 165 × 60 × 75 cm, part 3: 80 × 80 × 50 cm
Private Collection
[p. 42] *Slow Death*, 2009
Cast polyurethane resin, stitched and dyed canvas, acrylic paint, 31 × 11 × 6 cm
Anne Faggionato Collection, Monaco
[p. 43] *Survivors*, 2008
Cast polyurethane, bicycle parts, dimensions variable
Private Collection, New York
[p. 44] *Triptick*, 2011
Polyurethane resin, vinyl, 33 × 37 × 5 cm
Private Collection, New York
[p. 45] *Trip Over*, 2007
Epoxy resin, polyurethane foam, jesmonite, steel rod, acrylic paint, shoelaces, 69 × 28 × 15 cm
Martin & Rebecca Eisenberg Collection, New York
[p. 46] *Landfill*, 2010
Cast polyurethane, polyester resin, iron powder, 47 × 57 × 20 cm
Private Collection, London
[p. 47] *Power Lunch*, 2011
Polyester resin fiberglass, resin cast, 61 × 31 × 21 cm
[p. 49] *You'll be dead for years without even knowing it*, 2011
Polyester resin, fiberglass, resin cast, motorized water system, dimensions variable
[p. 50] *Washout*, 2006
Cast fiberglass, epoxy resin, 91 × 31 × 31 cm
Private Collection, Miami
[p. 51] *Phantom Bouquet (Lights Out)*, 2005
Cast fiberglass, flowers, 117 × 19 × 19 cm, edition 2 of 3
Private Collection, Geneva
[p. 53] *Bubble Head*, 2006
Plastic, plaster, metal rod, 50 × 23 × 18 cm
Tim Nye Collection, New York
[p. 54–55] *Alnight Row*, 2011
Polyester resin, varnish, enamel, acrylic paint; three parts, 33 × 9 × 10 cm each
[p. 57] *Grimewave*, 2011
Polyester resin, fiberglass, enamel, acrylic paint, 121 × 77 × 7 cm
[p. 59] *Prison Tattoo (2)*, 2011
Polyester resin, fiberglass, metal powder, spray paint, enamel, 83 × 46 × 25 cm
David Roberts Collection, London
[p. 60] *Gap Filler*, 2011
Polyester resin cast, fiberglass, 203 × 92 × 6 cm
[p. 63] *Invisible Idiot*, 2008
Smoke machine, dimensions variable
[p. 64] *Untitled (Flag)*, 2004
Resin, tape cassette, 10 × 17 × 2.5 cm
Private Collection, Glasgow

Courtesy: The Modern Institute/Toby Webster Ltd, Glasgow: cover, endpapers, 17, 20, 21, 22, 23, 24, 27, 29, 31, 32, 33t, 34, 35, 36, 37, 38–39, 41, 42, 43, 44, 46, 57, 59, 63, 64; Barbara Gladstone Gallery, Brussels: p. 1, 30, 33b, 44, 47, 49, 60; Anton Kern Gallery, New York: p. 2, 5, 7, 8, 9, 11, 12–13, 14–15, 26, 28, 45, 54–55; Michael Benevento, Los Angeles: p. 18–19; Sadie Coles HQ, London: p. 35, 43; Nils Stærk, Copenhagen: p. 50, 51; Ancient and Modern, London: p. 53

Photo Credits: Anna Arca: cover, 17; Ruth Clark: endpapers, 21, 22, 32, 34, 38–39, 42, 59, 63, 64; David Regen: p. 1, 30, 33b, 44, 47, 49, 60; Thomas Müller: p. 2, 5, 7, 8, 9, 11, 12–13, 14–15, 41, 45; Joshua White: p. 18–19; Anders Sune Berg: p. 20, 50, 51; Photographic Services: p. 23, 24, 36, 37; Simon Vogel: p. 26, 54–55; Serge Hasenböehler: p. 27; Tom Little: p. 28; Marcus Leith, ICA, London: p. 29; Aram Jibilian: p. 31; Andy Keate: p. 35, 43, 53; Prudence Cuming Associates Ltd: p. 46, 57

This book was published on the occasion of Richard Hughes' exhibition *Where It All Happened Once* at Tramway, Glasgow, 26 October to 16 December, 2012.

EDITORS Lionel Bovier and Clément Dirié
AUTHORS Martin Clark, Joanne Tatham
EDITING AND PROOFREADING Clare Manchester
ASSISTANCE Mélanie Borès

DESIGN Gavillet & Rust/Piguet, Geneva
TYPEFACE Hermes (optimo.ch)

COLOR SEPARATION & PRINT Musumeci S.P.A., Quart (Aosta)

The publication has received the support of Anton Kern Gallery, New York; Barbara Gladstone Gallery, Brussels; and The Modern Institute/Toby Webster Ltd, Glasgow.

All rights reserved. No part of this publication may be reproduced, stored in a retrieval system, or transmitted, in any form, or by any means, electronic, mechanical, or otherwise without prior permission in writing from the publisher.

© 2012, the authors; the artist; the photographers; and JRP|Ringier Kunstverlag AG

Printed in Europe

Published by
JRP|Ringier
Letzigraben 134
CH-8047 Zurich
T +41 (0) 43 311 27 50
F +41 (0) 43 311 27 51
E info@jrp-ringier.com
www.jrp-ringier.com

ISBN: 978-3-03764-239-9

JRP|Ringier books are available internationally at selected bookstores and from the following distribution partners:

Switzerland
AVA Verlagsauslieferung AG
Centralweg 16, CH-8910 Affoltern a.A.
verlagsservice@ava.ch, www.ava.ch

France
Les presses du réel
35 rue Colson, F-21000 Dijon
info@lespressesdureel.com, www.lespressesdureel.com

Germany and Austria
Vice Versa Vertrieb
Immanuelkirchstrasse 12, D-10405 Berlin
info@vice-versa-vertrieb.de, www.vice-versa-vertrieb.de

UK and other European countries
Cornerhouse Publications
70 Oxford Street, UK-Manchester M1 5NH
publications@cornerhouse.org, www.cornerhouse.org/books

USA, Canada, Asia, and Australia
ARTBOOK | D.A.P.
155 Sixth Avenue, 2nd Floor, USA-New York, NY 10013
dap@dapinc.com, www.artbook.com

For a list of our partner bookshops or for any général questions, please contact JRP|Ringier directly at info@jrp-ringier.com, or visit our homepage www.jrp-ringier.com for further information about our program.

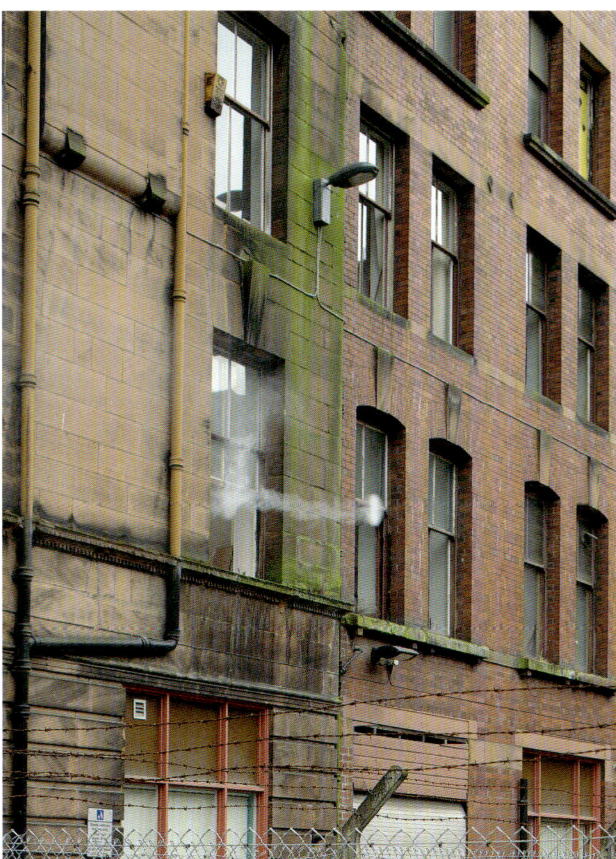

INVISIBLE IDIOT, 2008

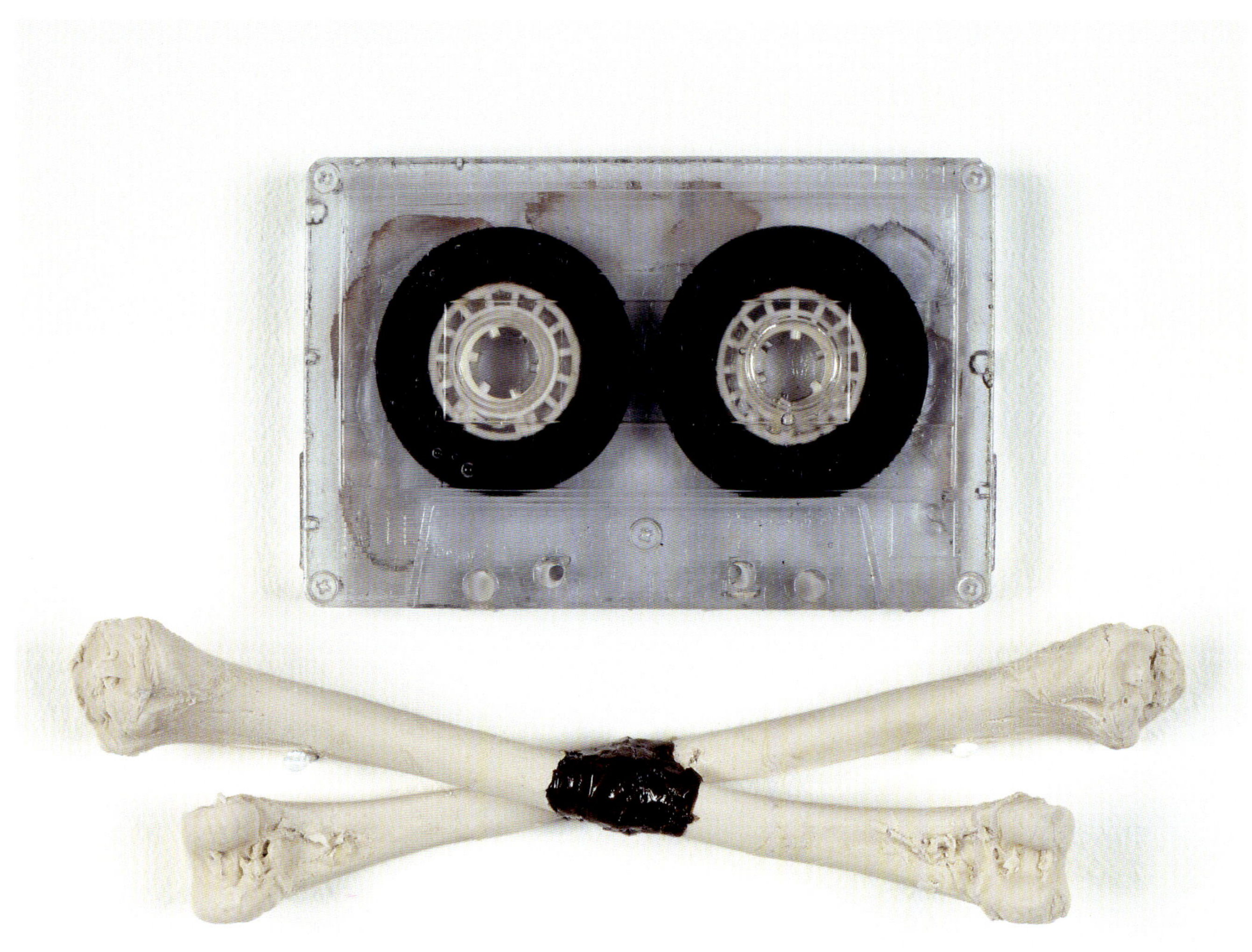

UNTITLED (FLAG), 2004

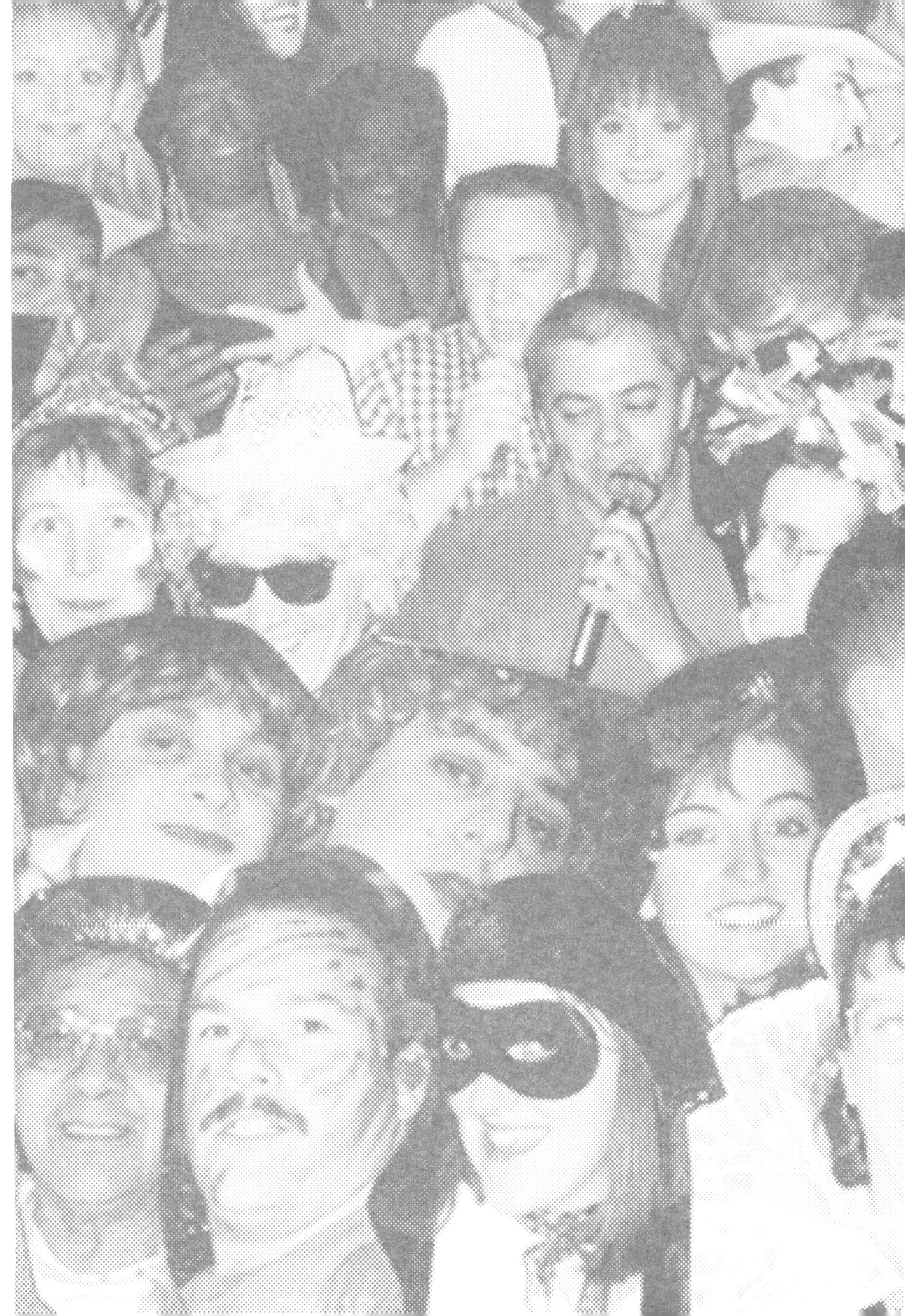

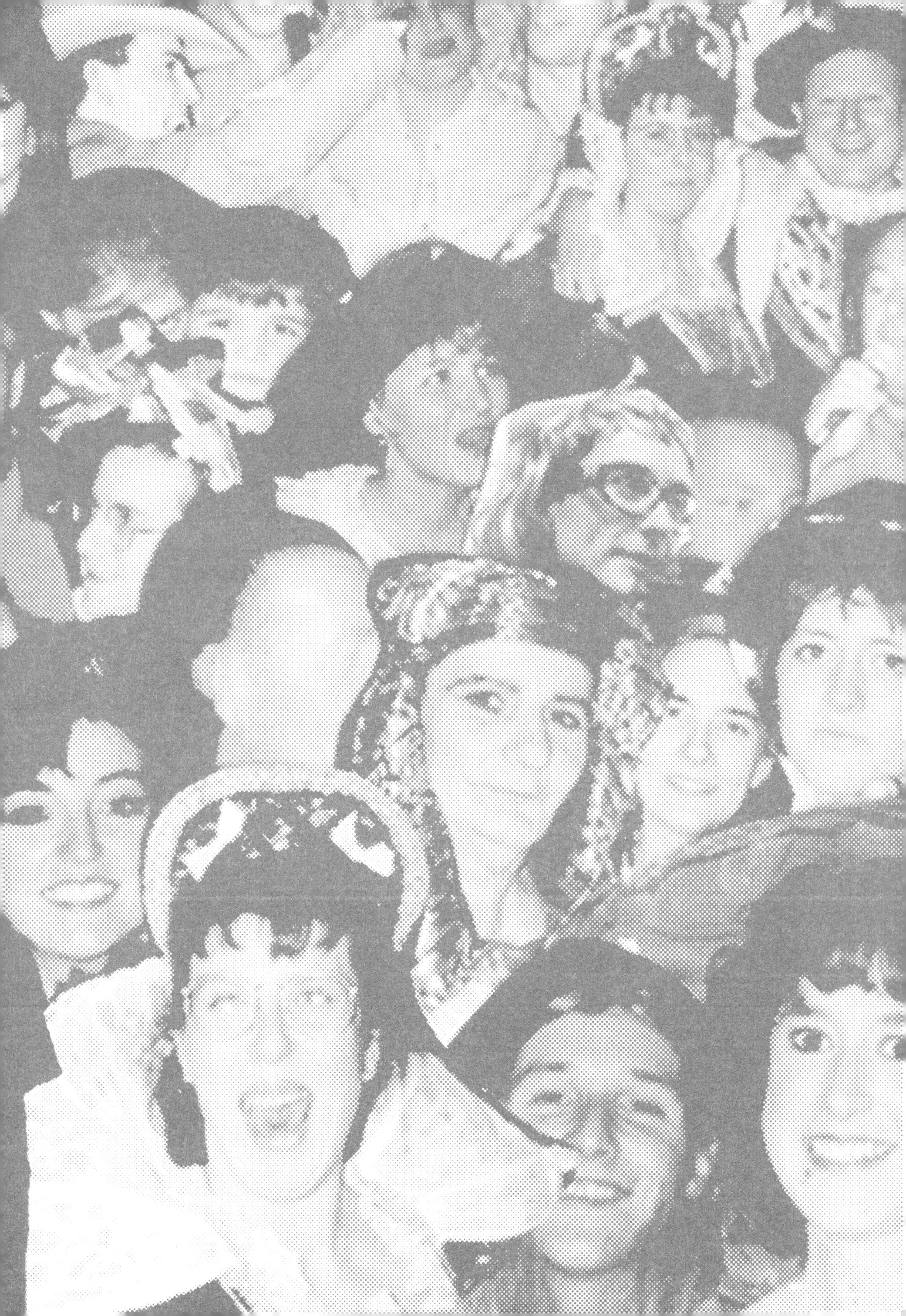